I ♥ STATIONERY

First published in 2012 by
Jacqui Small llp
An imprint of Aurum Press
7 Greenland Street
London NW1 0ND

Copyright © RotoVision SA 2012
www.rotovision.com

Art Director: Emily Portnoi
Cover design: Emily Portnoi
Design concept: Emily Portnoi
Artworking: Rebecca Stephenson
Commissioning Editor: Isheeta Mustafi
Photos on page 112 courtesy of Galison
Photos on page 142 by Lilian Day

Typeset in Mr Eaves and Museo Slab

ISBN: 978 1 906417 69 7

A catalogue record for this book is available from the British Library.

2014 2013 2012
10 9 8 7 6 5 4 3 2

Printed in China by 1010 Printing International Ltd.

I ♥ STATIONERY

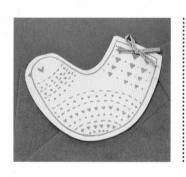

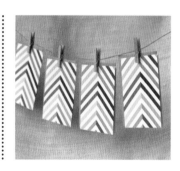

jacqui
small

CHARLOTTE RIVERS

CONTENTS

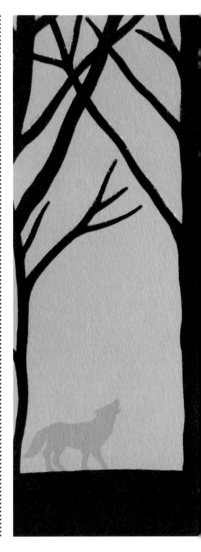

INTRODUCTION

Despite digital technology dominating the way we communicate and record information—from e-mailing to texting to blogging—the stationery industry today is thriving and is home to some of the most interesting examples of illustration and design, and creative artisan processes. It seems that despite the onslaught of digital media there are those who still like to indulge in the slower, more tactile medium of the handwritten letter or card, and they are matched by an abundance of designers, printers, and crafters creating stationery. As Jen Shaffer of Minnesota-based Painted Fish Studio explains: "I would like to think that people who buy my paper goods are those who value aspects of a slower way of life: instead of texting or sending an e-mail, they prefer to send a letter. They're writing their thoughts in a journal, not in a blog."

It is a testament to the many designers and crafters out there that the stationery industry is so strong. The market is huge, with a number of fairs and shows held worldwide, such as the National Stationery Show in New York. Recent years have also seen an increase in the popularity of craft and design markets, many of which incorporate stationery, such as the Finders Keepers markets in Australia. Of course the continued success of online market-places such as Etsy and Folksy, where much of the work shown on the pages of this book can be found, is further proof that the demand for handmade products from smaller practitioners is growing.

Throughout this book you will find work by designers from around the world, showcasing a number of different artisan processes. From screen printing,

block printing, illustration, letterpress, and more, the way in which each stationery item is made is as important as its actual design. For the purposes of this book, stationery includes greeting cards, notecards, writing paper, envelopes, wrapping paper, gift tags, calendars, journals, notebooks, diaries, and stamps. It has all been organized according to the technique or process used to create it.

Hand-drawn Illustration celebrates the abundance of stationery featuring original illustrations created by hand. Styles vary hugely, from simple pen-and-ink drawings to more complex works using gouache paint or digitally colored imagery. What they all have in common, however, is that any given illustrative style is unique to its creator—instantly recognizable as theirs.

Screen Printing explores the ways and means by which designers and printers use this technique to design stationery. Like other artisan printing processes, screen printing has seen a huge rise in popularity in recent years. It offers creatives an economical, hands-on way to print onto many different surfaces and materials. The Japanese Gocco printing system has also gained a huge following in recent times. Its manageable size and high-quality output make it an appealing choice for designers and printers, alongside traditional screen-printing methods.

4

5

It's hard to have missed the revival in the fortunes of *Letterpress Printing* in recent years. Presses that were once destined for the scrap heap have been restored and brought into designers' studios, and are now used to print the vast quantities of beautiful letterpress-printed stationery available today. From small runs printed on Adana tabletop presses to larger runs printed on Golding Jobber platen presses, this resurgence in popularity shows no sign of abating.

Block Printing is a lesser-used artisan craft, but it is slowly on the rise, and as the work in this chapter shows, there is a real skill in carving and creating blocks for printing. Although most artists today use linoleum for their blocks rather than wood, the method of carving, which has existed for hundreds of years, remains unchanged.

Digital Illustration takes us away from traditional artisan crafts and into a world that has transformed the way in which designers and artists are able to create imagery. Software such as Adobe Photoshop and Illustrator offers huge scope for image creation and manipulation—either solely or together with hand-drawn or scanned elements. This chapter includes work featuring both vector-based illustrations and "hand-drawn" digital illustrations, created freehand using either a mouse or a graphics tablet.

Firmly back within the world of the handmade, *Calligraphy* showcases the work of some of today's best-known contemporary calligraphic practitioners. Inspired by traditional calligraphic styles, or "hands," this chapter explores the ways in which today's artists are experimenting with those long-established styles to create innovative new work for today's design-conscious market. Calligraphy is no longer consigned to just wedding stationery. In its modern, contemporary forms, its uses are far more versatile.

Another ancient craft that has seen a huge increase in popularity in recent years is *Papercutting*. With roots as far back as the sixth century, this method of creating delicate, hand-cut imagery is fast being adopted by many of today's young creatives. Techniques differ but, as the work in this chapter shows, the results remain the same— quite simply, beautiful.

The final chapter covers work that includes *Collage, 3-D, and Sewn* elements. This is where that ever-popular term "handmade" really comes into its own. Some pieces feature the ancient Japanese art of origami, while others use mixed media ranging from fabrics to card to embroidery floss to buttons, and more, to create a truly eclectic mix of work.

Together these chapters cover a wide range of skills and techniques. I hope that the work presented in them serves to inspire and delight as well as to inform. The overwhelming quantity of work received and selected for inclusion in this book really goes to show how, even in this age of digital media, beautiful handcrafted paper goods still have their place.

Charlotte Rivers

TECHNIQUES &
PRACTITIONERS

CHAPTER 1

HAND-DRAWN ILLUSTRATION

Hand-drawn illustrations add something of a personal touch to a design, giving a piece that ever-popular handmade aesthetic. Styles vary considerably, but each artist will have their own unique approach, resulting, over time, in a signature style that can be recognized instantly.

Hand-drawn illustrations feature heavily in stationery design, and the techniques used to create them are many and varied. Most start with a pencil, or pen and ink, on paper. Some are left as simple line drawings; others are colored. Coloring may be done using dry media (such as crayons, colored pencils, chalks, or oil pastels), wet media (inks, watercolors, or gouache paints), or digitally, using Adobe Photoshop or Illustrator. Whether this last method is used or not, the process of taking a hand-drawn illustration to print will generally involve the use of digital technology at some point. In some cases an illustration will simply be scanned and imported into Adobe Photoshop, Illustrator, or similar software, "cleaned up," and then saved as a high-resolution image ready for printing. In other cases an image will be digitally enhanced. This could involve coloring, adding in other elements, incorporating this image into a wider design layout, or adding in lettering or type.

Hand-drawn illustrations are also printed using other methods, such as block printing, screen printing, and letterpress printing, each with its own process for creating print-ready imagery.

HAND-DRAWN ILLUSTRATION TOOLS

PAPER

The choice of stock will depend on the drawing implements being used. Standard sketchbooks containing 100lb (150gsm) white acid-free cartridge paper serve well for both pencil and pen-and-ink drawings, as well as paint. However, some illustrators like to use heavier specialist paper, with a variety of flat or textured surfaces, when working with watercolors, acrylics, gouache, or other paints to create color. Vellum paper and Bristol paper give different results with pens. Layout paper allows for the tracing and redrawing of images.

PENS

Brush or fiber tips, fine liners, roller balls, nib pens, markers, or Sharpies; the range of pens available is huge and the choice is personal. Illustrators tend to settle on the pen that they find most comfortable to hold and that gives them the application they desire.

PAINT

Typically, watercolor, acrylic, or gouache paints.

BRUSHES

Artists' paintbrushes come in a number of different shapes, sizes, and hairs (natural or synthetic). The ultimate brush is made using sable hair, although many synthetic brushes compare well.

PENCILS

Graphite or colored—again, the choice is wide and varied and illustrators tend to use pencils that are comfortable to hold and suited to their particular drawing technique.

SCANNER

Used to import hand-drawn imagery onto a computer in order to make it print ready.

AMYMARCELLA

MILWAUKEE, WISCONSIN, USA

Amy M. Soczka is a designer and illustrator working under the name of amymarcella. This calendar features her hand-drawn illustrations in a format that is an ode to her "obsessive list-making habit" and was printed on 100lb bright white cardstock. "I like to collect plant matter and flowers, always paying attention to the repetitive patterns and variegated lines in the details," she explains. "My botanical illustrations are a combination of any of these elements."

The cards are part of a series called Compliments and feature an exaggerated version of Amy's own handwriting. The goal of the series was simply to design cards that could be sent to "brighten up someone's day." The hand-drawn lettering was imported into Illustrator to be digitized and colored before being printed on 80lb recycled French Paper cardstock.

SUKIE

....

BRIGHTON, EAST SUSSEX, UK

Sukie was founded by Darrell and Julia Gibbs. They design and produce a variety of notebooks, accessories, and home furnishings for their own brand as well as working with other brands on design projects. "We focus on design that is conceptual as well as decorative, functional, and fun—and high quality, but affordable at the same time," explains Darrell.

Shown here are their notebooks, My First Novel and Note Book for Winners. Both feature hand-drawn illustrations and artwork. "We use various methods for our artwork," Darrell says. "They always start off as drawings. Then we make them into lino prints or give them texture by copying them on a fax machine. The final image is then put together on the Mac."

The notebooks were printed on recycled paperback card and paper stock.

SWISS COTTAGE DESIGNS

NEW YORK, NEW YORK, USA

Swiss Cottage Designs is run by Courtney Jentzen and is a custom design studio, specializing in stationery, invitations, and personal and corporate branding. "I have a strong background in illustration and like to incorporate hand-drawn elements in my work wherever I can," Jentzen explains. "I have an affinity with whimsical illustration and great typography."

Both of these greeting cards feature Jentzen's illustrations. For the Love card she drew the letters by hand in pencil before painting in the color using watercolors on a 130lb cold-press surface. For the Fort Greene card she drew the illustration by hand and then colored it in digitally using Photoshop.

DRAWCITY

CAPE TOWN, SOUTH AFRICA

South African graphic designer and illustrator Fayrooz Abader trades under the name of Drawcity.

All of Abader's illustrations are drawn by hand using black felt-tip pen. They are then imported into Adobe Photoshop so that color can be added; otherwise the original images are not digitally altered at all.

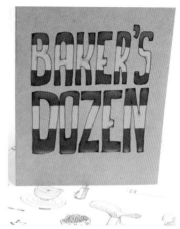

MAI AUTUMN

ASBURY PARK, NEW JERSEY,
USA

Christine Lindstrom is an artist and designer who works under the name of Mai Autumn.

"I wanted to capture a lovely sense of nostalgia in an item that could be used as an everyday luxury," she says of these vintage-style cards. "I think that stationery is a perfect vehicle for little daily reminders of our own memories and daydreams. These folk-art notecards were inspired by my childhood memories of the decorative art in my grandmother's home. Each design is a compilation of traditional floral motifs from the 1950s, '60s, and '70s."

The illustrations for the cards were created by Lindstrom using Italian watercolor paints on heavy watercolor paper.

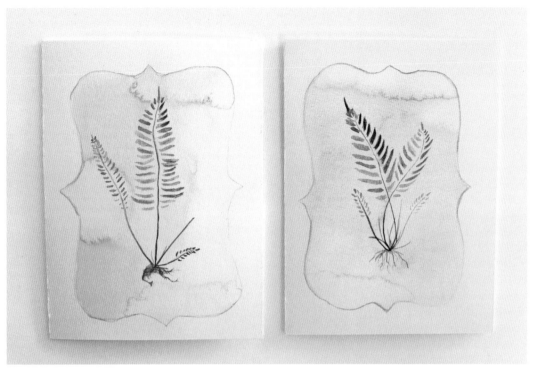

HEIDI BURTON

LONDON, UK

Heidi Burton is a freelance illustrator whose work is inspired by folktales, nature, music, literature, and poetry. Her output varies, from original illustrations, prints, handpainted ceramics, and altered Moleskine journals to greeting cards.

"My ethos is to create a positive and unique personal experience for each customer, with a handmade touch. My ongoing self-initiated brief is to create a series of altered journals with the theme of literature from around the nineteenth century. I read a lot of old poetry and folktales and my instinct as an illustrator is to respond to the text with drawings."

Burton works with Tombow double-ended pens or Rotring or Pilot fineliner ink pens. She also uses 2B or 3B pencils for her sketches and drawings. She applies color directly onto the paper using brush pens or watercolor paints.

PAPER & TYPE

LOS ANGELES, CALIFORNIA,
USA

Both of these products from
paper & type (see also pages 136
and 168) feature Victoria Vu's
hand-drawn illustrations.

The sketches for the This Year's
Flowers writing set span four panels
(or sheets), so a four-page letter
will yield a complete print. Vu also
added bright berry-colored lines
to the paper and included a supply
of aqua blue envelopes to counter
the grayness of the pencil sketches.

The Perpetual Planner features the
same hand-drawn flower illustrations
on both the brown paper cover and
the white inner pages.

ENORMOUSCHAMPION

NEW YORK, NEW YORK, USA

This company is run by photographer and letterpress printer Jordan Provost and graphic designer and illustrator Jason Wong. "We use recycled paper in our stationery, sustainably harvested wood in our animal silhouettes, and unbleached linen in our dishcloths. Everything is produced in the United States, and we use minimal cardboard and paper packaging for our goods," the husband-and-wife team explain.

Shown here are their Whale card box set and Fite-Cycles notecards. The whale illustrations are by Wong, while the Fite-Cycles are the work of Tim Fite.

The hand-drawn illustrations were imported into Adobe Illustrator and redrawn, ready to be made into photopolymer plates for printing on 110lb recycled cover stock.

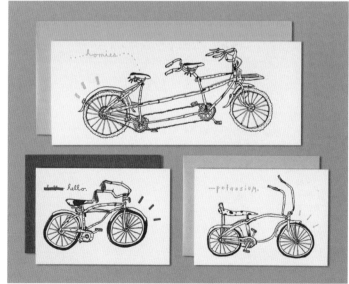

OH MY DEER HANDMADES

··

NASHVILLE, TENNESSEE, USA

Oh My Deer Handmades is run by artist and illustrator Chelsea Petaja.

Petaja's love of wreaths led to her designing this *Seasons of the Wreath* calendar, featuring her hand-drawn illustration and lettering.

The wreath in the center of the calendar mimics each of the seasons, going from spring to summer to fall to winter, and was handpainted using watercolors on smooth Bristol bright white cardstock. The illustration was complemented by the addition of handpainted lettering for the year and names of the months.

SUNLIGHT ON CLOSED LIDS

···

SALTAIRE,
WEST YORKSHIRE, UK

This is the work of Kate Holliday, founder and designer at Sunlight on Closed Lids. "I merge textiles, design, hand-drawn illustration, vintage patterns, and nostalgic imagery in order to form an original, colorful, energetic, and playful world within my stationery," she explains. "I offer heartfelt greetings, wise words, a story, personal message, words of love, or just a simple hello."

The illustrations shown on these greeting cards were created by hand, employing a variety of methods. "I like to use superfine black gel pens for the initial illustrations and enjoy using collage, colored pencils, gouache paints, and screen printing to create patterns and textures," she adds.

All cards were printed on Accent Antique white textured stock.

ANDY PRATT

NEW YORK, NEW YORK, USA

Andy Pratt uses a variety of techniques to produce his cards. These are a few of his Location Collection cards—Queens (New York), Seattle, Washington, and Vancouver; created during and after visits to each city.

The illustrations were sketched by hand before being scanned and inked in Flash and then colored in Illustrator using a tablet monitor. "Thus far all the cards in this series are of places I've been; in fact the Queens card was inspired by my commute on the subway from my old apartment," explains Pratt. "Recently I've been getting requests to illustrate cities I haven't yet had a chance to visit so for those cards I'll rely on photos taken by family and friends."

The cards were letterpress-printed on Crane's 110lb Pearl White Lettra cover stock.

JILL BLISS

PORTLAND, OREGON, USA

Jill Bliss is a freelance illustrator and designer. These are her hand-illustrated Sea Flowers postcard set and Succulent journals and stationery set.

"Before I begin each drawing I do lots of research—studying guidebooks, searching online, talking to naturalists, and making visits to a specific place with sketchbook and camera in hand," Bliss explains. "Everything is drawn by hand with pen and ink, then scanned into the computer to be put on various items, such as cards and journals. I add in the background colors digitally."

Each item in Bliss's line is printed with vegetable- or soy-based inks on 100 percent postconsumer recycled paper stock.

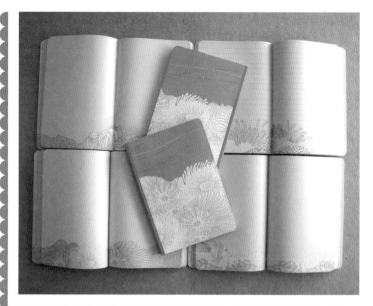

JO CLARK DESIGN
....

CAMBRIDGE,
CAMBRIDGESHIRE, UK

Jo Clark is an illustrator and designer. This is a selection of cards from her collection, which aims to celebrate the beauty of nature. "My designs emerge from organic shapes, with a sensitive use of line and a sophisticated color palette," she explains. "Inspiration for my flower designs comes from gardens and from train journeys to Norfolk, passing through countryside abundant in wild flora."

Clark works with graphite and pencils, pencil crayons, and marker pens. "I love to use marker pens for their versatility; they create an instant flat color and can also be layered to create depth and texture."

Final images are then scanned into Adobe Photoshop so that a card template can be created and sent to the printers.

KAROLIN SCHNOOR
LONDON, UK

Originally from Berlin but now settled in London, freelance designer and illustrator Karolin Schnoor creates the drawings for her card lines by hand before coloring and finishing them digitally.

Schnoor uses both digital printing and screen-printing for her cards. Shown here are her Folk Wolf, Folk Owl, Valentine, Thank You, and Cloak designs, all featuring her hand-drawn illustrations and type. Each card was printed on thick Fine Art Trade Guild (UK)–approved textured paper stock using archival inks.

LUCY KING DESIGN

MELBOURNE, VICTORIA, AUSTRALIA

Lucy King is a freelance illustrator and designer, originally from the United Kingdom but now living in Melbourne.

King has a background in textile and surface pattern design, having designed tableware for Wedgwood. She is now known for her muted watercolor florals and loose painterly style, although her artwork still often reflects her appreciation of vintage tableware: "I love to draw brightly painted florals, delicious cupcakes, and vintage china," she says.

Her mix-and-match line of cards incorporates all of these things. Each original artwork was created using Winsor & Newton watercolors and Arches watercolor paper, and then scanned and imported into Adobe Photoshop, where King created the final design. The cards were then digitally printed.

GEMMA CORRELL

BERLIN, GERMANY

Gemma Correll is a freelance illustrator and designer who creates stationery items, T-shirts, and tote bags. Her quirky hand-drawn illustrations are created simply using pen and ink. "I specialize in the fun side of the illustration spectrum, where the concept and use of words and humor are just as important as the image, if not more so," Correll says. "My work always has a narrative basis."

Both of these cards were created for a collaborative group project called "Love to Print" and were produced and sold for Valentine's Day. The original hand-drawn images were scanned and imported into Adobe Photoshop to be prepared for printing on a Gocco printer.

MELANIE LINDER / SPREAD THE LOVE

······································

FLEETWOOD,
PENNSYLVANIA, USA

Spread the Love is run by Melanie Linder, who designs and prints various stationery goods. "Love is my theme and happiness is my goal," she says. "I work in a spontaneous, whimsical way, dreaming up ideas or being inspired by music. This calendar was created as, after a few difficult years, I wanted to believe the next year would be 'my year' so I proclaimed this on the calendar I designed."

Linder drew the illustrations for the calendar by hand before importing them into Adobe Illustrator and adding typography to create the layout. The font used is called Folk and the calendar was printed on 80lb Wassau cardstock.

O-CHECK DESIGN GRAPHICS (SPRING COME, RAIN FALL)

SEOUL, SOUTH KOREA

O-Check Design Graphics produces a wide variety of stationery goods. "The name O-Check comes from the Korean word *gongcheck*, meaning 'notebook,'" explains designer Cho Su-Jung. "The aim of our brand is to evoke strong emotions and feelings of nostalgia. Our products are mainly printed with soy ink and made with eco-friendly materials, including recycled paper and linen."

The notebooks shown here all feature hand-drawn illustrations. Also shown are some of O-Check's Christmas decoration cards. These are designed to be sent as holiday cards that can then be made into decorations and hung up by the recipient.

ALLISON COLE
ILLUSTRATION
· ·
PROVIDENCE, RHODE
ISLAND, USA

Allison Cole is an illustrator who
works out of a former candy factory.
She creates products ranging from
paper products to soft goods and
accessories such as tote bags
and pillows.

The cards in the Bonjour card set
feature Cole's ink drawings. These
were scanned into Adobe Photoshop
where they were colored and
arranged ready for printing onto
thick coated cardstock. The imagery
for the hand-printed notebooks was
created and arranged in the same
way, but was screen printed by
hand onto recycled cardstock.

KRISTIN CARLSON

MOSCOW, IDAHO, USA

Kristin Carlson is a printmaker working primarily in screen printing and mixed media. "Much of my work is inspired by the look of written correspondence and letterforms," she explains. "Some of my printmaking work also uses imagery based on maps and architecture from places I have lived."

This postcard set features past and present iconic buildings in the city of Providence. The image of each building was first created on board using drawing, watercolors, and collage. The text for the reverse side was hand-lettered on a separate sheet. Then the sheets were scanned and manipulated in Adobe Photoshop to achieve the appropriate contrast and color before being digitally printed as double-sided cards using soy-based inks.

CHAPTER 2

SCREEN PRINTING

A screen print is created by passing ink through a screen containing a stencil onto a given substrate. The process can be used to apply artwork to many different surfaces, from paper and card to cotton, wood, or canvas.

Like letterpress printing and other artisan crafts, screen printing is currently enjoying a revival. It hails originally from Asia—particularly China and Japan, where it has been widely used from as far back as the tenth century. Despite its popularity in Asia, it wasn't widely adopted in Western Europe until the early twentieth century, when it began to be used to print wallpaper, linens, and silks.

Screens are created by stretching a piece of finely woven mesh material within a solid frame. Stencils are usually made using the photo-emulsion technique. A copy of the original image is created on a transparent overlay such as acetate, ensuring that the areas to be inked are opaque. The printer then selects a mesh screen, coats it in photo emulsion, and allows it to dry in the dark. Once dry, the overlay holding the artwork is placed over the screen and exposed to ultraviolet light, which passes through the clear areas of the overlay and hardens the emulsion on the mesh screen. The screen is then washed so that the unexposed

areas of emulsion dissolve and wash away, leaving the stencil in place. To print, ink is pulled down over the screen and pressed through the threads of the mesh onto the substrate.

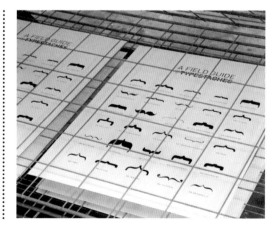

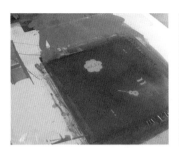
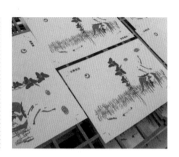

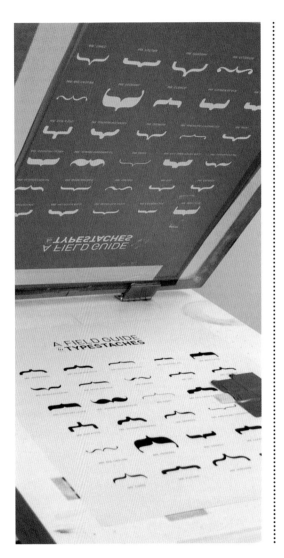

Print-ready stencils can also be created using the block-out method or the original cut-stencil method. For the first, the printer draws around the negative areas of the artwork with a glue-based solution, thus blocking the ink flow to these areas when printed. The second method sees the positive area of the image cut out of paper, leaving only the negative area. This is then secured to the screen so that the ink flows only through the areas of the screen not covered by the stencil, i.e., the intended image.

In addition to traditional screen-printing methods, the Japanese Gocco printing system is often used. It serves more as a craft method than an industry standard, but it has gained an avid cult following within the design and printmaking community. A Gocco press provides a superfine level of detail within images, produces great results with metallic and fluorescent inks, and allows complex multicolor split-fountain designs, which means several ink colors can be used at the same time. Gocco's parent company, Riso Japan, no longer produces the machines; however, its fans are now experimenting with other more readily available alternatives.

SCREEN-PRINTING TOOLS

PRESS

There are three common types of screen-printing press: flatbed, cylinder, and rotary.

INK

Solvent-, plastisol-, and water-based inks are the most commonly used.

FRAME

A wooden frame is used to hold the screen in place over the substrate. It is held high when the ink is applied and lowered when ready to print. Aluminum frames are also available; these are more resistant but also more expensive.

STENCIL

An image of the artwork, today created most commonly using acetate.

SQUEEGEE

This rubber-bladed tool is used to press the ink evenly through the mesh screen.

PHOTO-SENSITIVE EMULSION

A liquid that is applied to the mesh screen, enabling the creation of a stencil when it is exposed to ultraviolet light.

CORRUPIOLA
••••••••••••••••••••••••••
SÃO JOSÉ, SANTA CATARINA,
BRAZIL

Corrupiola creates *experiências manuais*, or "handmade experiences," and is run by artist and designer Leila Lampe and writer and web designer Aleph Ozuas (see also page 50 and page 95). Everything they create is carefully made by hand.

This selection of recycled mininotebooks was made from paper that was left over from the creation of other notebooks for their line. The mininotebooks feature a series of screen-printed, open-source dingbat images. Colored Fabriano Tiziano paper was used for the covers, and 80gsm Pollen Paper from Suzano for the signatures. Both papers are acid free.

Also shown here is their Golden Box, which features notebooks with fabric covers and silk-screen-printed covers, all housed together in a papercut recycled-cardboard sleeve.

HEART ZEENA
∙∙∙∙∙∙∙∙∙∙∙∙∙∙∙∙∙∙∙∙∙∙∙∙∙∙∙∙∙∙∙∙∙∙∙∙∙
LONDON, UK

Zeena Shah, who makes handmade goods using locally sourced materials, founded and runs this stationery and home accessories company (see also page 152). To reduce the impact of her business on the environment, she uses organic and recycled materials, and water-based dyes.

Shah specializes in hand silk-screen printing, but will often work by turning her drawings into papercuts and then using these to create new designs. These are her A Birdie Called Bob greeting cards, Birdie gift tags, Wonderous wrapping paper, and Nigel notebooks. The notebooks and wrapping papers have screen-printed covers, which were inspired by Shah's love of sewing and cross-stitch.

All items were screen printed and the Nigel notebooks feature hand-stitched binding.

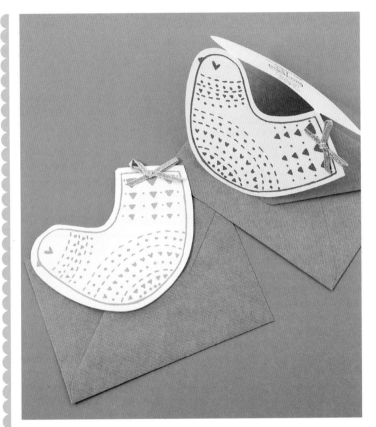

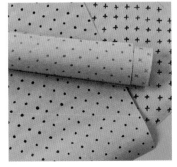

CORRUPIOLA AND THEREZA ROWE

SÃO JOSÉ, SANTA CATARINA,
BRAZIL / LONDON, UK

This illustrated notebook is the result of a collaboration between Brazilian designers and printers Corrupiola (see also page 46 and 95) and the London-based designer and illustrator Thereza Rowe (see also page 133). It was inspired by a love of cats, shared by both Rowe and the Corrupiola duo.

The illustrations were created first as rough pencil sketches and then drawn in more detail using a graphic tablet and Adobe Illustrator. "I like the flexibility of working with vectors," explains Rowe. "You can draw freely without worrying so much about size or dimensions, since vectors can be blown to any size without loss of quality."

The notebook was screen printed by hand on acid-free Pollen 90gsm stock for the body and Duo 300gsm design paper for the cover.

LA RARA

SYDNEY, NEW SOUTH
WALES, AUSTRALIA

This limited-edition, screen-printed
stationery company is run by
Lara Raymond.

Raymond creates her designs in
Adobe Photoshop and/or Illustrator,
using a mix of vintage and modern
illustrations and typography.
Each of her stationery items is then
thermally imprinted on a screen
before being hand-printed using a
Gocco printer and original Japanese
Gocco inks in limited runs.

"The cards are made from start to
finish in the same room. It is a very
immediate process—reassuringly
time-consuming but with beautiful
results," she explains. "Each item is
truly unique and slightly different
from the others, which I love."

ME AND AMBER

SYDNEY, NEW SOUTH
WALES, AUSTRALIA

Karen Enis and Amber Molnar
are the duo who run this company,
producing a variety of handmade
items, from housewares to stationery.
Their designs feature simple, bold
silhouette graphics, illustrations,
and typography.

"We love everything to do with
greeting cards—not just their design
or their physicality, but also the
meaning associated with them.
The act of giving and receiving
a card is really special, particularly
in this age of e-mail and digital
technology. As we've always loved
notebooks, they were a natural
progression when we wanted to
expand our line of greeting cards."

All of these cards and notebooks
were printed on recycled paper
using the old-fashioned stencil
screen-printing technique.

NORA WHYNOT PAPER GOODS

BRISBANE, QUEENSLAND, AUSTRALIA

This Australian company produces a variety of paper goods using environmentally responsible materials and 100 percent recycled card and paper. Much of their work features hand-drawn or digital illustrations, and all their products are silk-screen printed except, as shown here, the bookplates and garden journal, which were printed by offset lithography.

The design of the perpetual calendar was inspired by old wives' tales and features specially created illustrations. The cooking folders, decorated with silhouette illustrations, were created using heavy box card and are part of the "Nora says... File it!" collection of boxboard folders, as is the ruler folder.

HELLO JENUINE

DUNDEE, ANGUS, UK

Hello Jenuine is Jen Collins, an illustrator who often employs screen printing to complement her illustration work (see also page 150).

Collins created the illustrations for these notebooks by hand using brushes and inks. She then screen printed each cover before hand binding the cover and inner pages together.

Both the cover and paper inside are made from recycled stock.

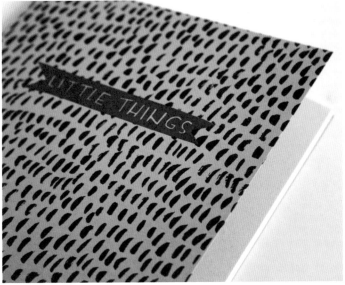

MORRIS & ESSEX

LIMINGTON, MAINE, USA

Morris & Essex is a stationery company run by designer and printmaker Eliza Jane Curtis (see also page 87).

Curtis printed these greeting cards in her home studio using the traditional (large-format) silk-screen process. She used hand-cut stencils and a combination of Rubylith film and thick black construction paper to make the design and burn the silk screen.

"I have a very hands-on aesthetic that comes from a love of tactile crafts; I seldom use the computer," she explains. "Designs combine my love of historic ornament and decorative ephemera and memories of childhood daydreams in the fields and forests of Maine to create motifs of geometry, fantasy, and nature."

ANJA JANE

LONDON, UK

This print company, run by Anja Jane Sheriden, specializes in printed textiles and screen prints as well as greeting cards. "I love color and pattern and try to incorporate as much as possible into my products," Sheriden explains. "I screen print all my paper products in my London studio. It is so wonderful in a digital age to step away from the computer and mix real paints and work physically to create images."

This Owl card was created from a limited-edition screen print. The image was first drawn in pen and ink and then scanned and tidied up to be made into a screen. It was then screen printed using two layers.

W+K STUDIO GOODNESS
....
PORTLAND, OREGON, USA

Goodness (see also page 82) is a side project of the Wieden + Kennedy graphic design studio. When not making ads, the creatives there design T-shirts, calendars, greeting cards, posters, and more.

This calendar features the work of twelve different designers and was created with the aim of showcasing a wide range of talent from the studio within a functional object. Each designer was asked to create artwork for a given month, the results of which see a mix of hand-drawn illustrations, vector art, and type.

The calendar was screen printed in black and white on French Paper brown paper stock.

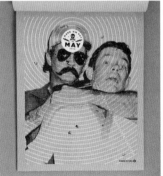

AKIMBO

....

ADELAIDE, SOUTH
AUSTRALIA, AUSTRALIA

Akimbo is run by graphic designer
Alicia Parsons, who designs invitations,
cards, and other stationery items.
This is her Woodland collection,
which features a fill-in invitation,
Christmas card, gift tag, and food
flag. The collection was commissioned
by Mary & Gabrielle Events and
Poppies Flowers.

"The theme was a rustic Christmas
with oak leaf details and a palette
of berry and natural materials,"
explains Parsons. "The natural
woodsy details inspired the oak leaf,
acorn, and squirrel motifs that I then
screen printed by hand in white onto
brown packaging paper. I just love
the solid color that can be achieved
against a dark paper."

ACUTE & OBTUSE
....

SEATTLE, WASHINGTON,
USA

Acute & Obtuse is husband-and-wife team Heidi and Jose Rodriguez. They enjoy working with recycled materials and exploring multiple printing techniques and processes.

This series of cards was created with the intention of making interactive products that could also be shared. "We wanted to create something that both the giver and the receiver could keep a piece of. We brainstormed and out popped the wishbone and popsicle," explains Heidi.

The cards were silk-screen printed and then perforated so that they can be torn and shared.

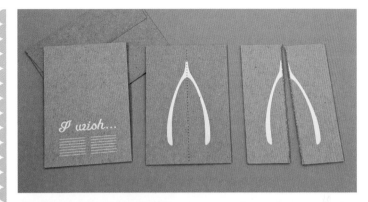

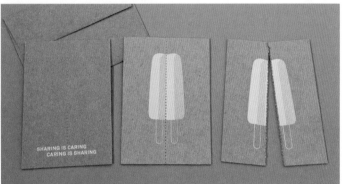

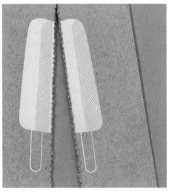

SAKURA SNOW

AMSTERDAM,
THE NETHERLANDS

Suzanne Norris (see also page 151) is an artist and designer. In addition to working on client-based design projects, she creates a line of stationery and paper goods for her Sakura Snow store.

These are her A Wolf and Bear in a Winter Wood greeting cards. "I wanted to make a card design that would exude a sense of peace and equilibrium as an antidote to all the 'festive craziness,'" she explains. "A forest after a heavy snowfall is a magical place—still and tranquil—and I hoped to convey something of this peacefulness in this simple design."

The cards were screen printed in two colors on off-white 220gsm Hahnemühle acid-free card. The designs wrap around both the front and back of the cards.

CABIN + CUB

VANCOUVER, BRITISH
COLUMBIA, CANADA

Cabin + Cub is run by Valerie Thai and specializes in art direction, print design, and illustration for nonprofit, socially conscious, and sustainable companies. Thai also designs and prints a stationery line.

The artwork for these notebooks was inspired by vintage children's book illustrations from the 1950s, '60s, and '70s. The illustrations were drawn by hand before being imported into Adobe Illustrator and then burned onto Print Gocco screens. These were then screen printed onto the notebooks using the Gocco printing machine.

CHAPTER 3

LETTERPRESS PRINTING

This form of relief printing was, for many years, the primary method of printing for the masses. During the 1960s, however, it was somewhat superseded by offset lithography printing, save for a small number of specialist printers who continued to champion it.

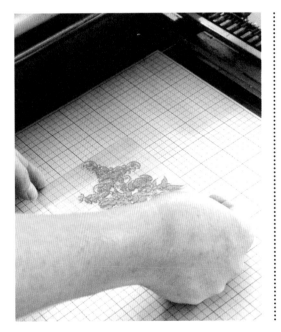

In recent years, though, this unique and much-loved printing method has seen something of a resurgence in popularity as an increasing number of individuals and small companies are setting up shop and producing letterpress materials and goods.

Letterpress printing works by setting type, plates, or blocks in a chase and placing them on a printing bed. They are then inked and a relief print is made on paper or card. How this happens depends on the printing press itself. Presses range from small tabletop models to larger hand-fed models, such as the Chandler & Price or Golding Jobber platen presses, and presses with automatic feeds, such as the Heidelberg Windmill and the motorized Heidelberg KSBA flatbed cylinder press.

There are a number of ways to create artwork for letterpress printing. Designs can be created by hand using metal or wood type and blocks; lead type is hand set using a composing stick whereas wood type, which tends to be larger, is set in a chase directly on the printing bed. Alternatively, artwork can be created digitally and transferred onto a plate ready for printing. Hand-carved linoleum blocks can also be used on some presses.

LETTERPRESS-PRINTING TOOLS

PRESSES

There are various kinds of printing presses available. For the smaller printer a tabletop model such as the Adana 8x5 and/or a foot-operated platen press such as a Chandler & Price will suffice. For those wanting to produce a larger volume or size of work a Heidelberg Windmill or Vandercook flatbed press will serve better.

METAL TYPE

The individual letters and punctuation marks used in traditional letterpress printing. The main material used is lead.

WOOD TYPE

Wood type can be used together with, or instead of, metal type. It is often used on a large scale and has today become a highly collectable item.

PLATES

Printing plates, or blocks, are created from digital or hand-carved artwork and are typically created using zinc, magnesium, copper, photopolymer, or hand-carved linoleum blocks. A different plate will be created for each pass of color required for a particular design. All can be used on printing presses as long as they are "type high" (as high as the standard height of type, which is $^{15}/_{16}$in [23.3mm]).

INK

Water-soluble rubber-based or soy-based inks are the most popular inks today. Inks can be either used straight from the can or mixed to produce a particular shade or color. Use ink sparingly—one spoonful will go a very long way.

COMPOSING STICK

A metal instrument used to assemble individual pieces of metal type into words, lines, and sentences in preparation for printing.

QUOINS

These are small locks that are used within the printing chase to lock and secure it ready for printing.

KEY

A T-shaped tool used by a printer to tighten up quoins in the printing chase.

ROLLERS

Rollers come in all shapes and sizes and are found on all presses. They take the ink and pass it on to the type or block ready for printing.

EGG PRESS

PORTLAND, OREGON, USA

Egg Press is known for producing inspiring handcrafted letterpress greeting cards and other paper goods. They were one of the pioneers in driving the current resurgence in the popularity of letterpress printing. Egg Press create stationery both for their own lines as well as taking on commissions.

Shown here is a calendar, plus a selection of cards from their Valentine line. All feature hand-drawn illustrations created using brush pens and typeset messages and dates. The cards and calendars were printed either on a Vandercook or Chandler & Price press using Mohawk Superfine Ultra White stock with Van Son Rubber Base inks.

THESE ARE THINGS

COLUMBUS, OHIO, USA

These Are Things—run by designers Jen Adrion and Omar Noory—were famed initially for their simple, modern, letterpressed world maps. They now produce other paper items, including the *This Year's Adventures* calendar and Fill in the Blank card sets shown here.

"Our design process is super collaborative," Noory explains. "We pass the piece back and forth digitally until we're happy with the final product, then it's off to the print shop."

They work with Allison Chapman of Igloo Letterpress, translating each of their digitally designed pieces to beautiful letterpress-printed items using a Vandercook no.4 proof press and Johnson Peerless platen press with Van Son Rubber Base inks.

SEESAW DESIGNS

SCOTTSDALE, ARIZONA, USA

This creative studio, run by Angela Hardison, Raquel Raney, and Lindsay Tingstrom, works on brand identity and other graphic design projects for various clients. They also produce a letterpress stationery line.

The illustrations for the calendar and cards were all created by hand before being scanned and traced digitally for letterpress printing.

The calendar features both letterpressed elements and foil stamping in rose gold. Both were printed on Crane's Lettra 110lb (300gsm) stock using Van Son Rubber Base inks and a Kluge platen press.

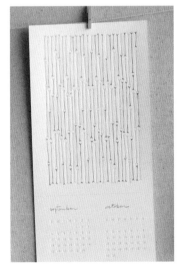

PAPERSHEEP PRESS

NEW YORK, NEW YORK, USA

Papersheep Press is run by Gina Houseman, who combines photography and graphic design to create letterpress stationery.

Houseman's projects often begin with a photograph or drawing that is then inputted into design software and layered with design elements before being made into a polymer plate ready for printing. She uses Crane's Lettra 110lb (300gsm) stock when wanting to make impressions, or Ecru colored paper. "I love the tactile quality of letterpress printing and strive to let the impression shine as much as possible," she explains. "I do this by often utilizing the blind impression technique."

The designs for these notecards were inspired by her surroundings, and each was hand printed.

1CANOE2

COLOMBIA, MISSOURI, USA

This stationery company is run by Beth Snyder and Carrie Shryock, who print their designs using two antique Chandler & Price letterpresses. "We try and concentrate on creating happy, fun work with a focus on hand-drawn illustrations as opposed to computer-generated artwork," they explain.

These letterpressed recipe and address cards were printed on French Paper 140lb cardstock and come with homemade wooden boxes. The Thank You cards feature hand-drawn illustrations created using pencil, paper, and ink. The cards were printed on Crane's Lettra 110lb (300gsm) stock in Fluorescent White using Van Son Rubber Base inks.

INK+WIT

••

FAYETTEVILLE,
NEW YORK, USA

INK+WIT is run by designer and illustrator Tara Hogan.

Every year Hogan designs a limited-edition calendar. Her 2010 *Beings and Places* calendar was inspired by trips to Iceland, England, and France. Bold shapes, lines, and vintage colors form the overall aesthetic.

The 2011 *Totem Animals at Play (Pulling the Weeds, Planting Good Seeds)* calendar was inspired both by her research on totem animals and by the yogic phrase "Pull your weeds, plant good seeds." "This phrase captures how we need to weed our mental garden and manifest goodness in order to be truly happy," she explains.

All designs were sketched in pencil and then drawn in Adobe Illustrator before being sent to a letterpress printer and printed on Crane Lettra stock using a Vandercook press.

OLD TOM FOOLERY

MINNEAPOLIS, MINNESOTA, USA

Old Tom Foolery was founded by Lauren Weinblatt and Joel Gryniewski, based on their appreciation for letterpressed goods and their desire to produce a series of cards that expressed their dry sense of humor.

"Our tagline is 'Unsappy, uncrappy greetings and more,' which pretty much sums up our philosophy," explains Weinblatt. "We want to make premium-quality products that are surprisingly witty."

These cards are from the Footnotes collection and were created with the aim of appealing to both men and women. The idea was for them to be witty cards with a clean, simple design.

The cards were printed on a cylinder press by San Francisco–based Dependable Letterpress using Van Son Rubber Base ink and Reich Paper 118lb (320gsm) Savoy Natural White stock.

Thanks a million.*

*Must you always be so goddamn nice?

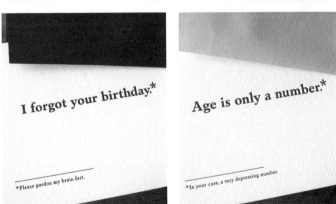

I forgot your birthday.*

*Please pardon my brain fart.

Age is only a number.*

*In your case, a very depressing number.

SESAME LETTERPRESS

NEW YORK, NEW YORK, USA

Sesame Letterpress is a Brooklyn-based print shop. Their work is influenced by the Victorian era, the period from which their presses date. They are inspired by etchings of nineteenth-century advertising cuts and botanical and animal illustrations. "We share the Victorian fascination with nature, etiquette, taxidermy, and other curiosities," explains founder Breck Hostetter, "and we've found a niche by pairing this vintage imagery with contemporary design and bright colors."

Each of these pieces was printed by hand on their circa 1890 Golding Jobber press. The stock used is either 110lb Strathmore or Manila cardstock.

"We love the idea that, in this digital age, we create something beautiful that passes from our hands to a client's hands, to their friend or loved one's hands, sometimes traveling around the world to do so."

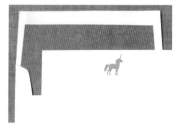

HAPPY BIRTHDAY

I LOVE YOU

HAPPY BIRTHDAY

CHEERS

THE HUNGARY WORKSHOP

BRISBANE, QUEENSLAND, AUSTRALIA

This collaborative letterpress and design project was set up by Simon and Jenna Hipgrave. "What excites us about letterpress is controlling the entire process from concept to execution," says Jenna. "We believe there is a little more to letterpress than a smart typeface with a rich color and a deep impression."

All of their cards have a unique twist. Their Bye Bye Beard is a quirky Valentine's Day card for (real) men. No printed "love" or hearts, but plenty of love in the gesture and heart in the sentiment.

All the cards were printed on a Heidelberg Windmill platen press using hand-mixed Van Son Rubber Base inks and Stephen Smart White 330gsm Australian-made, 50 percent recycled stock.

MAY DAY STUDIO

MONTPELIER, VERMONT,
USA

May Day Studio is a bookbinding and letterpress studio whose roots are in traditional letterpress techniques, including hand-set metal, wood type, and hand-carved linoleum. They also ensure that they use the most eco-friendly papers and inks in their studio.

Shown here are a number of their greeting cards, all of which were printed using linseed-oil inks on 100 percent cotton Stonehenge paper on the studio's Chandler & Price 8x12 or Vandercook SP15 printing presses.

Also shown is their Square Journal. The decorative cover papers are original May Day designs and were printed on the Vandercook SP15 using hand-carved linoleum blocks and linseed-oil inks.

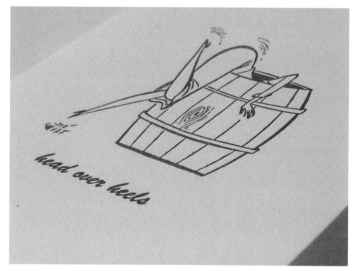

JESSE BREYTENBACH

CAPE TOWN, SOUTH AFRICA

These cards by printmaker Jesse Breytenbach (see also page 108) were designed in collaboration with Cape Town letterpress printers Planet Press.

"With these cards I wanted to design something that I wouldn't be able to carve and print myself so as to exploit the letterpress's ability to reproduce fine lines," Breytenbach explains. Her original pen-and-ink drawings were scanned and vectorized ready for printing on a Heidelberg platen press using Van Son Rubber Base inks.

CODY HALTOM

AUSTIN, TEXAS, USA

Cody Haltom is a designer working in art direction, visual identity, print and interactive design, and illustration. He is also a founding member of Public School, a creative collective composed of designers, illustrators, and photographers.

This is his business card design for Crimson & Whipped Cream, a bakery and coffee bar located near the University of Oklahoma. Old recipe cards served as rough inspiration and Haltom took the design in a more modern direction. The cards were letterpressed by Vertallee Press on Neenah Classic Crest Natural 130lb cover stock in order to give them a stronger tactile feel. The shape was then created using a custom die-cut. Hand-drawn type for the cards was created by Will Bryant.

W+K STUDIO GOODNESS

·······················

PORTLAND, OREGON, USA

Goodness is a side project of the Wieden + Kennedy graphic design studio (see also page 59).

Their Warm Fuzzies and Embroidered card series were both letterpress-printed on Crane's 110lb Pearl White Lettra stock using a Chandler & Price 10x15 press. The Warm Fuzzies collection was inspired by vintage crochet and knitting patterns, while the Embroidered series takes its inspiration from cross-stitch patterns and charts.

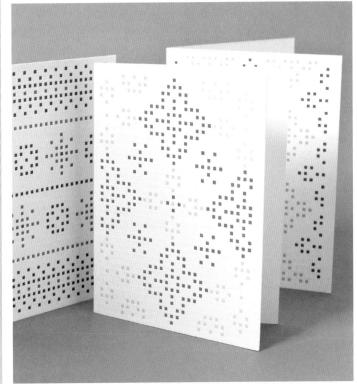

HAMMERPRESS

••••••••••••••••••••••••••••••••••

KANSAS CITY, MISSOURI,
USA

This U.S. letterpress and design
company runs three Vandercook
Universal I presses, a Heidelberg
Windmill, and a number of
Chandler & Price presses. These
greeting cards were created using
their substantial letterpress type
and ornament collection.

"We have grown to a store of
four full-time people and we work
collaboratively, bouncing our ideas
off one another," explains designer
and founder Brady Vest. "Our design
process begins with doodles and
sketches, then some of our designs
are created directly on the press,
while others will be created digitally
prior to printing."

All of their cards are printed by
hand on 30 percent or 100 percent
recycled stock.

SPRING OLIVE
....
CHICAGO, ILLINOIS, USA

Spring Olive is owned and run by graphic designer, illustrator, and letterpress printer Olivia Samson. "I've always had a passion for creating with paper and ink, from Crayolas and paint-by-numbers to ballpoint pens and printer ink," she explains. "Spring Olive bloomed from this passion, and my mission is to create cheery, optimistic pieces that bring a smile and warm the heart."

These greeting cards feature Samson's hand-drawn illustrations and were letterpress printed on an antique Vandercook no.4 proof press using Van Son Rubber Base inks. Samson used various paper stocks, including Crane's Lettra 100 percent fluorescent white and 100 percent cotton pearl white, and French Paper's super thick Whip Cream and Mod-Tone Taupe paper.

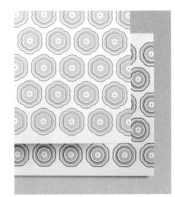

KIRTLAND HOUSE PRESS

CHICAGO, ILLINOIS, USA

Kirtland House Press produces vintage-style greeting cards, note-cards, ready-to-write invitations and announcements, calendars, prints, and gifts—all letterpressed by hand on an antique Vandercook press.

"Kirtland House Press began out of a passion for design, paper, and all things vintage, especially antique Vandercook presses!" explains designer and principal Kerrie Kirtland. "We find delight in mixing ink by hand to create the perfect hue, cranking a freshly kissed design off the press, and feeling the crisp, deep impression on a luxurious cotton sheet."

They digitize vintage printer cuts by scanning them and using Adobe Illustrator and InDesign to create fresh designs. They then make polymer plates of these designs to print with. All products are printed on 100 percent tree-free paper made from recycled fibers.

MORRIS & ESSEX

LIMINGTON, MAINE, USA

These letterpress-printed greeting cards are the work of Eliza Jane Curtis (see also page 57).

"I work with an old-fashioned master printer near my hometown in Maine, who prints on an impressive collection of beautiful antique letterpress machines," she explains. "I design with pencil and paper, then have metal plates engraved for printing."

The cards were printed on French Paper's Whip Cream 100lb paper stock, using custom-mixed Patriot oil-based inks.

JOIE STUDIO

PASADENA, CALIFORNIA,
USA

Joie Studio is a boutique artisan design and letterpress studio producing custom and ready-made letterpress products on a Golding Pearl Improved platen press and a Vandercook no. 4 Old Style precision proof press.

These Cheeky Faces cards were produced in collaboration with Shop Toast, a Hawaii-based custom favor company that is heavily influenced by J-pop and Asian-style animation.

Also shown here is Joie Studio's 2011 *Exotic* calendar, which was inspired by classic Asian design, art, and textiles. It has been printed on eco-friendly bamboo paper to complement the Asian designs.

DWRI LETTERPRESS

····································

PROVIDENCE,
RHODE ISLAND, USA

Shown here is a collaborative calendar project between Dan Wood of DWRI Letterpress and Alec Thibodeau. "Tiny Showcase asked Alec to come up with a design for a lunar calendar (now four years running) and decided to print it on a letterpress," explains Wood. "Alec creates amazing ink portraits of people, places, and things, which were the inspiration for this piece."

The calendar was printed using a mix of polymer plates, and hand-set lead type for the blind debossed titling and numbering. To create moons that would glow on the yellow paper, the moon plate was run through the press three times and then overprinted with a glow-in-the-dark varnish. The stock used was Smart Papers Passport Marigold 80lb cover.

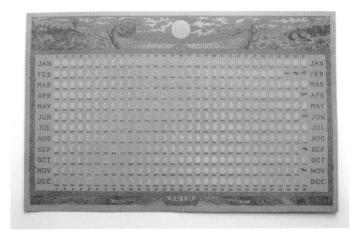

WINGED WHEEL

••••••••••••••••••••••••••••••••

TOKYO, JAPAN

Winged Wheel is a Japanese
stationery company specializing in
cards, letter sheets, and envelopes,
with stores in both Tokyo and Osaka.

Shown here are two of their notecard
lines, each of which has been printed
on 100 percent pure cotton paper
that is exclusively produced at the
foot of Mount Fuji. The illustrations
for the cards were created by hand
and then letterpress printed.

SNAP + TUMBLE

TORONTO, ONTARIO,
CANADA

Snap + Tumble is run by Tanya Roberts out of her home studio in Toronto. Her specialty is printing original, small-sized letterpress goods in short runs. These are her Homemade Journals and Lined Envelopes.

The journals feature letterpress-printed type and were made with a simple binding technique, using a cover-weight cardstock, bond paper, waxed thread, an awl, and bookbinding tape. The envelope liners were created using paper from rolls of vintage wallpaper that Roberts found in thrift stores. The notecards within the envelopes feature handset 12pt Franklin Gothic metal type and were blind printed.

NATASHA MILESHINA / BUBBO

NEW YORK, NEW YORK, USA

As well as working as a designer, Natasha Mileshina runs a company called bubbo, producing stationery, organizers, and notebooks. Products feature custom-made calligraphy and mostly use recycled materials. "My clients tend to be creative people who appreciate a clean, simple aesthetic and custom-made products, and love to keep their notes and thoughts in the 'old school' way—on paper rather than digitally," she explains. "They often come by looking for a special gift for their friends or significant others."

Shown here is her Valentine's Day gift wrapping set, which was inspired by cross-stitch embroidery, and her Etsy shop identity, which was inspired by old wax seals. Both items were letterpress printed using soy-based inks.

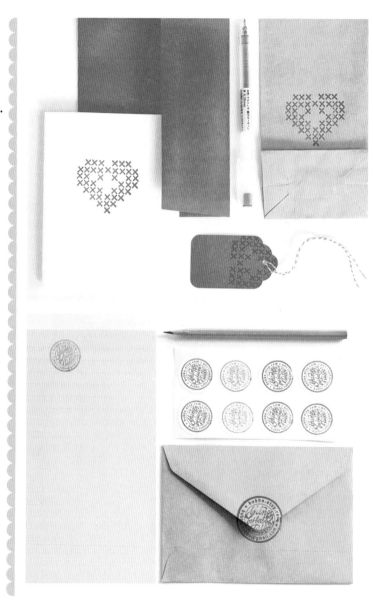

CORRUPIOLA

SÃO JOSÉ, SANTA CATARINA, BRAZIL

These letterpressed notebooks were inspired purely by the letters and numbers that Corrupiola (see also pages 46 and 50) bought with a letterpress printing machine. The designs for the covers were all created directly in the letterpress galley.

Once the covers were designed and printed, the signature pages were added and the books were then hand-sewn together. The types used were Grotesca Reforma Preta Estreita and Grotesca Larga Meia Preta and the press was a restored Minerva machine. The cover stock is brown packaging paper while the signature pages are Pollen Paper from Suzano.

CHAPTER 4

BLOCK PRINTING

Block printing is a form of relief printing that involves carving designs directly into a chosen surface—wood, linoleum, cork, rubber, vinyl, or even foam. It originated in China and India, where it has been used for centuries to print images and patterns onto fabric.

A printer will carve a design into a solid block using tools such as a veiner, awl, chisel, or carving knife. Designs can include text or be purely visual. A predetermined design or pattern can be drawn onto the block prior to carving, or the artist can carve freehand into the block.

Once the design is completed, the surface of the block is inked ready for printing by hand onto the chosen substrate. Alternatively, the block can be mounted so that it is type high (see page 67) and then locked up and printed using a letterpress. Blocks can also be attached to acrylic or wood for better stability and control when stamping.

Since wood can be quite challenging to work with, linoleum is often the preferred choice for creating a block. It is far softer then wood and thus easier to carve. However, it provides enough resistance to allow precise cuts, which results in crisp details, and produces a block that is better for registering multiple stampings. Rubber is less popular, but its softness and flexibility make it very easy to carve.

Water- or oil-based inks can be used, but traditional block printing is done with natural dyes. In order to print a design with multiple colors the printer will need to carve a separate block for each color, making sure they fit together exactly. Most traditional textile prints have three or four colors, so these would have required a block for the background, outline, and fill color of each design. A block that is well cared for can be used repeatedly for different projects.

BLOCK-PRINTING TERMS AND TOOLS

BLOCK
Block printers carve patterns and designs in a range of different materials, with linoleum tending to be the most popular.

VEINER
A gouging tool, usually with a U- or a V-shaped cutter. A veiner cuts thick, deep lines or "veins" that create larger relief spaces when the cuts are overlapped. Veiners also produce tapered lines.

CHISEL
This is a carving tool with a small, usually flat, metal tip and a narrow handle. Some chisels have blades; others have gouge tips.

KNIVES
Both fine-edged carving knives and utility knives are used to create intricate detail on blocks. Knives used for block printing can have rounded edges, flat edges, or sharp pointed tips, and are often small, with a cutting edge of an inch or less.

REGISTRATION
Ensuring multiple blocks line up on one print.

AWL
An awl has a mushroom-shaped narrow handle and a sharp, pointed tip that can be used to mark a block without cutting it. Awls are used to create tiny dots in a design.

ROLLER
An important tool for block printing, the roller—also called a brayer—is used to apply ink to the finished block for printing.

BARREN
A barren is used to transfer the ink from the block onto the paper. It has a wide, flat surface and a handle. The artist places the paper against the back of the block and applies pressure while moving the barren in a circular motion.

PALETTE
Used to hold paint or ink while working. Glass sheets are popular for this purpose.

ANNA FEWSTER / LAMPYRIDAE PRESS

....

BRIGHTON, EAST SUSSEX, UK

Anna Fewster runs a small block-printing and letterpress studio on the south coast of England, producing custom-made and ready-made stationery under the imprint Lampyridae Press. Her work is greatly inspired by the decorative interiors and printed designs of the Bloomsbury Group. The designs for these cards were hand cut into linoleum blocks. The blocks were then mounted and printed layer by layer using an Adana 8x5 platen press with linseed oil printing inks from T. N. Lawrence. "I like the painterly quality you can achieve with linoleum blocks; something that is difficult to get with more 'perfect' materials such as photopolymer plates," Fewster says.

The corresponding envelopes were lined by hand with acid-free tissue paper in complementary colors.

KATHARINE WATSON

WASHINGTON, D.C., USA

Katharine Watson specializes in block printing by hand on both fabric and paper using a hand-carved linoleum block.

"After studying printmaking I went to India and did an apprenticeship at a block-printing factory, spending hours sitting cross-legged on the floor learning to chisel tiny wood blocks," she explains. "Now I combine the two techniques—linoleum printing and Indian block printing—to create my own style of work."

The greeting cards and notebooks here feature designs that have been inspired by the patterns found in textiles, architecture, and nature. "I'm drawn to floral and geometric patterns, and I love the way block printing enables you to take a very delicate pattern and make it bright and bold."

TUESDAY DESIGNS

MELBOURNE, VICTORIA, AUSTRALIA

Tuesday Designs is a collaboration between sisters Taryn and Elise Eales. "Elise and I have always made little bits and pieces together since we were tiny, so it seemed completely natural to build on our childhood games and make-believe and start Tuesday Design," says Taryn. "We also share a love of birds, which continues to be a thread in our work."

The sisters created these block-printed bird cards by first sketching out some ideas, then transferring them to linoleum and chiseling out the design. The blocks were then blind embossed. "I soaked a heavy art paper and blind embossed the image on the block under heavy pressure and blankets using an etching press," Taryn explains. The stock used was Hahnemühle 380gsm, a heavy German etching paper.

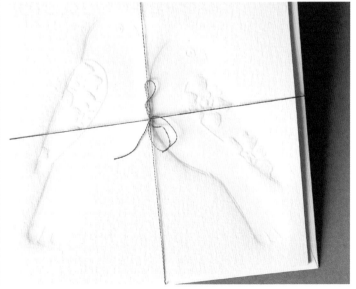

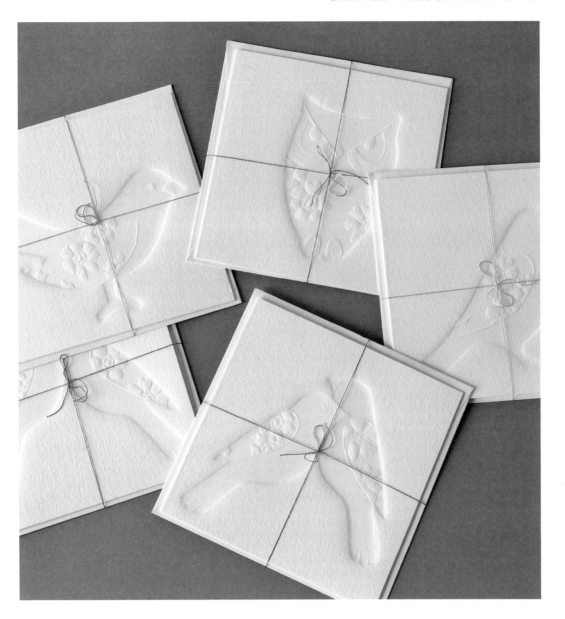

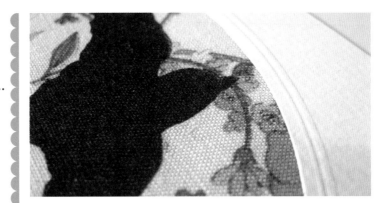

HAVE & HOLD DESIGN
....
TORONTO, ONTARIO,
CANADA

Have & Hold Design was founded
and is run by Samantha Dubeau
(see also page 175). "My business
began with one simple idea: life
should be celebrated," she explains.
"When holidays and momentous
occasions occur it's an opportunity
to celebrate. My pieces honor this
and are meant to be cherished and
held on to."

Shown here is her Treasures of
Yesterday collection of cards. Each
one was block printed by hand.
"I designed this line of cards for
anyone who appreciates the antique
aesthetic," Dubeau says. She began
by making digital mock-ups of her
designs before carving them into
rubber blocks. The designs were then
printed onto found vintage fabrics
and, finally, glued inside the framed
cards. "As with many of my other
works, I wanted something that
incorporated the sense of touch,"
Dubeau adds.

FIELD GUIDE DESIGN

KINGSTON, NEW YORK, USA

Field Guide Design is run by artist and designer Darbie Nowatka from her home in upstate New York. This is a sample of her hand-printed wrapping paper. "I had picked up some old Indian hand-carved wooden printing blocks at a yard sale because I loved the patterns and wanted to make something beautiful with them," she explains. "I took them home where I made hundreds of individual prints with black printing ink on plain white paper before scanning the best of the bunch into Photoshop to create my patterns."

Nowatka had a large silk screen made to print the final pieces with opaque water-based fluorescent inks on 100 percent recycled brown paper. "I was able to make something that had the beauty and imperfections of hand printing with a much higher level of consistency than I would have been able to achieve using the blocks as they were originally intended."

PINE STREET MAKERY

NASHVILLE, TENNESSEE,
USA

Pine Street Makery is run by
Jessica Maloan, a native Tennessean.
Following an internship at letterpress
print shop Hatch Show Print, where
she learned how to incorporate her
linocut illustrations with wood and
metal type, Maloan started selling
her linocut greeting cards and prints
on Etsy and in small stores.

Shown here are her Valentine Teepee
cards, Microscope card, and Travel
Camper card. The artwork for each
started life as a sketch, before Maloan
carved it into a linoleum block ready
for printing. Each was printed on
Paper Source A2 cardstock.

RUBY VICTORIA LETTERPRESS & PRINTMAKING

....

HOBART, TASMANIA, AUSTRALIA

Ruby Victoria is run by Narelle Badalassi, who specializes in linocut and letterpress printing. Her designs are drawn by hand, then carved out of linoleum blocks or hand set using letterpress type before being printed on an Adana 8x5 tabletop press.

"I make prints because I enjoy the process. I find carving an image in lino very calming and I can get lost in the process for hours. The only other thing I like as much as carving is seeing the first print pulled from the block."

For her Merry Christmas notecards and gift tags, Badalassi wanted to create something clean and classic. The heart design was hand-carved and the cards and tags created using 36-point Bodoni bold lead type.

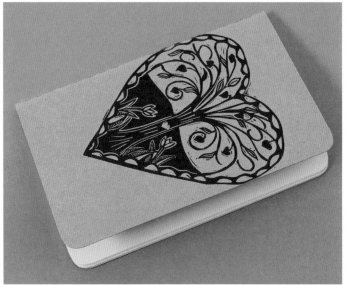

JESSE BREYTENBACH

CAPE TOWN, SOUTH AFRICA

Jesse Breytenbach (see also page 80) uses carved linoleum blocks to produce both fabrics and papers, and prints on her kitchen table using a rolling pin and sometimes an old bookbinding press.

"I try to work as simply as possible, producing small runs at a time," she explains. "My primary aim is not to waste; I try to use every scrap of fabric or paper. For instance, my gift tags are printed on leftover pieces from my greeting cards."

The illustrations for these gift tags were first drawn in pencil, then carved into a linoleum block ready for printing using Van Son Rubber Base inks. The illustration for the block-printed fabric portfolio case was first hand drawn, scanned, and then finalized digitally. This too was carved into a linoleum block, then printed using water-based inks on leftover scraps of fabric.

CHAPTER 5

DIGITAL ILLUSTRATION

Digital technology has transformed the way designers and illustrators create artwork. Most creatives tend to work using Adobe Illustrator or Photoshop, as these programs are the most comprehensive on offer, with seemingly endless features and options, while InDesign can be used for multipage designs.

Artwork can be created in a variety of ways—the most popular is to draw freehand or to draw using vector graphics. The latter involves using geometrical shapes, lines, and curves to create images and patterns. Vector graphics are created using mathematical formulae, as opposed to pixels, which means that any given image can be scaled to any size and detail without pixelating, and that you can move, rotate, and align objects easily to achieve your desired look. However, if you require more freedom, or a more hand-drawn aesthetic, you can use a mouse or graphics tablet. These digitally mimic traditional hand-drawn methods. In addition to Adobe Illustrator and Photoshop, programs such as Studio Artist contain freehand drawing–based tools that allow artists to replicate pastel, watercolor, or chalk drawings. Digital technology is also used to add color or manipulate hand-drawn imagery.

DIGITAL ILLUSTRATION TERMS AND TOOLS

ILLUSTRATOR
A vector-based drawing program popular with digital illustrators for images and layouts.

PHOTOSHOP
A graphics-editing program used to manipulate photographs and imagery and assemble layouts.

INDESIGN
Software used for creating page layouts.

STUDIO ARTIST
A painting and graphics application with a huge range of brushes.

GRAPHICS TABLET
This allows freehand drawing digitally, using a graphics tablet pen and, in some cases, your finger.

DIGITAL PRINTING
Photo printers that use archival inks print well and on many types of paper, even up to thick chipboard stock. Since they use up to eight different inks, good color range and increased vibrancy can easily be achieved.

BRIE HARRISON
....
IPSWICH, SUFFOLK, UK

This is textile designer and illustrator Brie Harrison's Berry Field Collection for New York–based stationers Galison. Inspired by gardens and nature in general, her repeated pattern format is reminiscent of fabric and textile design.

Harrison starts by sketching out her ideas with a fine liner. She then scans her drawings and continues to work on them in Adobe Photoshop, experimenting with colors, details, and patterns to create her final designs. She uses a Wacom pen and tablet and various digital brushes.

DARLING CLEMENTINE

OSLO, NORWAY

Darling Clementine is a Norwegian stationery company run by designers Tonje Holand and Ingrid Reithaug. As well as creating designs for their own stationery line, they work on commissions.

Shown here is their Folk and Flora line of cards, the illustrations for which were drawn in Adobe Illustrator. "This line was inspired by the aesthetics of our Scandinavian upbringing," Reithaug explains. "We wanted to create a series of cards that had a cozy atmosphere and depicted life here."

The cards were digitally printed on 300gsm paper.

ALYSSA NASSNER

PHILADELPHIA,
PENNSYLVANIA, USA

Alyssa Nassner works as an illustrator and, together with screen printer and graphic designer Christopher Muccioli, also runs Small Talk Studio. The studio creates paper goods and simple home accessories, including screen prints, art prints, card sets, notebooks, notepads, and throw pillows.

As an illustrator, Nassner has worked with clients such as Chronicle Books and DwellStudio, as well as *UPPERCASE* and *Canadian Family* magazines. Some of her digitally created illustrations are shown on these pieces. The artwork for the Garden To Do pad was inspired by her houseplant collection. This, and the artwork for the Pencil notebook and Christmas card set, was created using Adobe Illustrator.

GIGI GALLERY

SAN FRANCISCO,
CALIFORNIA, USA

Gigi Gallery is a paper goods, design, and illustration store run by designer Gabriela Silva. Silva specializes in pattern and typography, and she is inspired by different cultures and by the handmade.

Silva's Monogram letter set and Native blue and red cards were inspired by Navajo culture and pattern; the Gracias card reflects her interest in typography, and the Weave cards display her love of color and pattern.

The designs were all created using pen and ink before being scanned and finished in Photoshop and Illustrator.

Each card was printed on French Paper's 140lb Speckletone in Starch White and comes with a Speckletone brown paper envelope. Both of these are postconsumer, recycled materials.

WIT & WHISTLE

∙∙∙∙∙∙∙∙∙∙∙∙∙∙∙∙∙∙∙∙∙∙∙∙∙∙∙∙∙∙∙

CARY, NORTH CAROLINA,
USA

Wit & Whistle is run by designer and maker Amanda Rae Wright, who produces illustrated greeting cards and paper goods. "I illustrate all my products—sometimes by hand and sometimes digitally," she explains. "It is very important to me that only the products I love and am proud of bear the Wit & Whistle name."

The digital imagery for these cards and notebooks was created in Adobe Illustrator using a Wacom tablet. Each item was digitally printed on recycled speckled paper or brown paper cardstock that was milled using clean, renewable hydroelectric energy.

Wright prints her cards herself, which gives her complete control over the production process. She uses archival-quality, pigment-based inks that resist fading and are very water resistant.

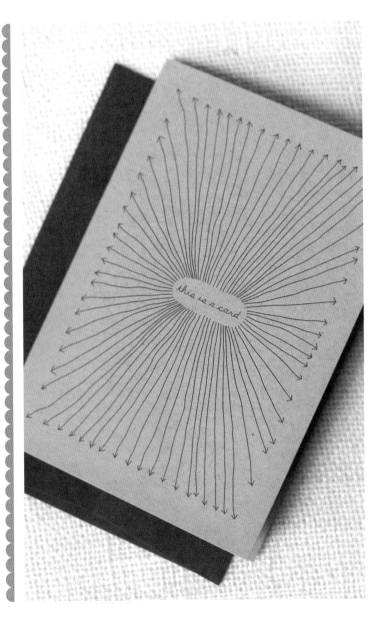

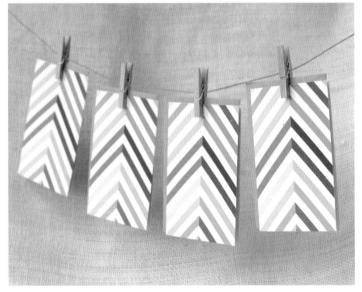

CRICICIS DESIGN

BOSTON, MASSACHUSETTS, USA

This paper goods and illustration company is run by Leah Ammerman. Her work has a minimal aesthetic, with an emphasis on clean, bright digital illustrations. "Many of my illustrations are of actual objects that you might find in my workspace, like cats or airport chairs," she explains.

Ammerman mostly uses Adobe Illustrator to create the drawings for her notecards and notebooks, although some illustrations begin life as hand-drawn sketches. All of the items shown here were printed on Neenah Paper cardstock.

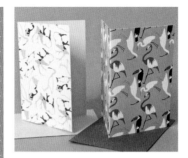

THE INDIGO BUNTING
....
NEW YORK, NEW YORK, USA

The Indigo Bunting is run by Erin Jang who creates unique, one-of-a-kind designs with modern illustrations and details. This is one of her calendar designs.

"I wanted to make something that I would want to hang in my home and something I could share with friends and family," she explains. "I aimed for a design that would feel timeless yet modern and brainstormed different icons that could work for each month. I then illustrated each month accordingly."

The clean, bold illustrations were created digitally and then type was added in Merriam and Futura. The calendar was four-color printed with a matte finish.

NANCY & BETTY STUDIO

CANTERBURY, KENT, UK

Nancy & Betty Studio is run by husband-and-wife team Andy and Hannah Bidmead. "Our designs are whimsical with bright colors and have a 'pretty tomboy,' retro feel to them," Hannah explains. "We like putting a bit of British in there too, as well as a good pun. Photography is a key part of our designs. They are then manipulated in Photoshop and applied to a product or design."

All artwork for the goods they produce is created digitally. All cards are printed on 300gsm white matte Forest Stewardship Council (FSC)–certified card using vegetable-based inks. The wrapping paper is printed on 90gsm FSC-certified recycled matte paper and postcards are printed on 280gsm matte cardstock—both also using vegetable-based inks.

ONE FINE DAE

SEATTLE, WASHINGTON,
USA

One Fine Dae (see also page 177) is run by Linda-Thuan Pham, a designer, crafter, photographer, and traveler. "Paper is my main medium. Sometimes, I will also throw in thread or fabric to complement what I'm doing with the paper," she says, "but paper comes first."

Her Bon Voyage postcards were inspired by primary colors and her love of traveling. "I first sketched the designs on the computer, then printed them on cardstock," explains Pham. "I used a craft knife to cut the shapes of each design, then placed these cutout templates on brown paper chipboard and painted over them with acrylic paint. The process is a bit cumbersome, but it allows each card to have its own, unique, and subtle differences. These postcards have a very nostalgic quality; they remind me of summers when I was young."

PRESENT & CORRECT

....

LONDON, UK

"We love anything stationery/office-based so the Present & Correct brand is an extension of that—an excuse to hunt for new and vintage wares as well as design our own products," explains Neal Whittington of Present & Correct. "Inspiration comes from old ephemera we have collected—anything to do with education, midcentury children's books and pamphlets, mail and stamp-based articles."

The illustrations, geometric patterns, and designs for their Geometry Set notebooks and Crown card were created using Adobe Illustrator. The Crown card can be folded up and worn as a crown.

SMOCK PAPER

SYRACUSE, NEW YORK, USA

Smock Paper is a stationery and letterpress company that prints on sustainable bamboo and 100 percent postconsumer recycled papers. It is a member of Green America's Green Business Network and also takes part in a number of other green initiatives. All printing is entirely wind powered.

This selection of wrapping paper, printed with digital illustrations designed by Amy Graham Stigler, was inspired by a combination of things—vintage fabrics, 1940s poster art, vintage sheet music, Henri Matisse, and Milton Avery.

MERRY DAY

BANGKOK, THAILAND

Merry Day is run by freelance designer and illustrator Pavinee Sripaisal. "I produce cute and whimsical illustrated paper goods," she says. "All items originate from my daily doodles, which are scanned and digitally finished using Adobe Illustrator. I print the goods myself using my own inkjet printer. That way I can control the color quality and more easily experiment with different kinds of paper."

This is Sripaisal's Simplicity Flower Greeting card set. "I want to make a set of flower greeting cards that look fresh and bright yet modern and cute at the same time," she explains. "Something that makes one feel good just looking at it."

FLOWERMILL

CAPE TOWN, SOUTH AFRICA

This stationery company is run by its founders Robyn van der Toorn, Deborah Inkson, and Ingrid Blohm. "We saw a gap in the market for a locally designed and produced stationery line and decided to take the plunge," van der Toorn explains. "Now Flowermill has become something of a design escape for us."

These wrapping paper samples feature bold shapes and patterns, all created digitally, inspired by tumbleweed, wild flowers, and gypsy damask. "The design challenge was to create continuous patterns that would work on a cylinder, as we printed sheets flexographically," she adds. "Flexographic printing creates a stamp so the outlines are not sharp but appear a bit wobbly, which adds to the feel of the paper." Each was printed on Sappi Platinum 85gsm.

REDSTAR INK

SAN DIEGO, CALIFORNIA, USA

REDSTAR ink is a handmade paper goods company started by designer Marcie Hicks. The design emphasis is on a clean aesthetic and personal organization, producing products that are simple, bold, and modern. "In an age of computers and hand-held technology, we celebrate the tactile quality of paper," explains Hicks. "There is something satisfying about checking items off a list or opening a piece of mail from a friend."

Featured here are Hicks's Honey Do, Left Brain/Right Brain, and Bills notebooks, and her *One* calendar, all of which combine clean digital typography with the company's handmade aesthetic. All were printed and produced using 100 percent recycled paper stock and chipboard covers.

SCOUT BOOKS

PORTLAND, OREGON, USA

Scout Books is a publishing platform that allows users to create custom notebooks and book projects. Researching new ideas back in 2009, Pinball Publishing had spotted a gap in the market for a notebook that their customers could design themselves.

Each book is offset printed using one or two spot colors on uncoated and recycled board and paper stock. All the typography and illustrations are created digitally, and all the inks used are made from plant oils such as soy, canola, safflower, and corn.

"The scout book is a customizable print format that has an endless number of uses," explains designer Nicole Lavelle. "It has become much more than a notebook as our clients devise innovative ways to use it."

JHILL DESIGN

BOSTON, MASSACHUSETTS,
USA

This graphic design studio is owned
by Jennifer Hill. She creates patterned
prints based on imaginary vacations
that she then uses to create greeting
cards and calendars. "Each initial
pattern I create is initiated by a simple
detail—for example, tiled mosaics in
Isfahan," she explains. "I then research
a city for more inspiration, with the
aim of capturing the essence of
a place within my illustrations."

Hill first sketches out ideas before
moving to the computer, where
she designs her final patterns using
Adobe Illustrator.

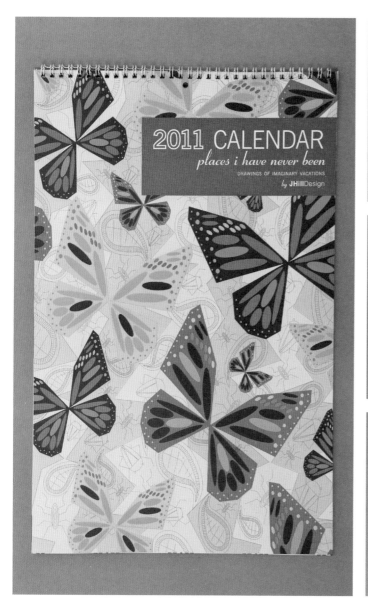

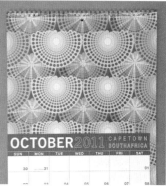

LOX+SAVVY

SYDNEY, NEW SOUTH
WALES, AUSTRALIA

Lox+Savvy is a Sydney-based
stationery and paper goods maker.
Founded by Lisa Loxley, the company
produces a whole array of items,
including wrapping paper, notecards,
pencil blocks, paper pockets, and
gift tags.

"After running my own design
studio and freelancing for years
I had a yearning to start up my own
stationery business," Loxley explains.
"While creating scribbles and designs
over a couple of years of some ideas
I had, Lox+Savvy was conceived."

With a love for bold, pastel, and
fluorescent colors, much of the
Lox+Savvy line has a strong, colorful,
graphic look. Each product was printed
digitally on recycled or carbon-neutral
paper, and all envelopes were folded,
glued, and finished by hand.

THEREZA ROWE

LONDON, UK

Illustrator and graphic designer Thereza Rowe (see also page 50) uses a variety of media to create her illustrations—from Adobe Illustrator to collage to papercuts and ink.

The illustrations on Rowe's Gatos card are of her own cats. The illustrations were created using ink on paper and were then imported into Adobe Illustrator to be finished and rendered. "Black ink and paper is how my ideas usually come about," she says. "It's always a starting point. Then I scan images and play with them in Photoshop."

The Hello cards were created using illustrations and cutouts from found paper. The type on the postcards was also hand drawn and edited in both Adobe Photoshop and Illustrator.

CHAPTER 6

CALLIGRAPHY

Calligraphy is an ancient form of handwriting and lettering that has existed for thousands of years. It is still popular today—both in its traditional forms and in more modern, adapted styles, as contemporary practitioners experiment and innovate with those long-established traditions.

Different calligraphic styles are described as "hands," and these hands are categorized according to the type of pen or nib used to create them. Broad-edge pen alphabets, for instance, include hands such as Foundational, Unical, Gothic, Versals, Neuland, and Bone, to name a few. Pointed-pen alphabets include Copperplate and Spencerian, as well as a number of contemporary pointed-pen styles. Brush alphabets use scripts created with flat and pointed brushes.

In addition to the traditional pens and nibs, some practitioners work with felt or ballpoint pens to create a more modern aesthetic. Nevertheless, they still tend to draw inspiration from the traditional hands. The choice of stock to write on is an important and highly personal one. Calligraphers either experiment with different varieties to achieve a range of results or settle on a preferred favorite.

CALLIGRAPHY TOOLS

PENS
A calligrapher can choose between traditional nib pens, which are dipped in inks; or pens that have built-in ink cartridges.

DIP PENHOLDERS
Used to hold calligraphy and drawing nibs.

NIBS
Nibs are attached to penholders and come in a range of shapes, including round hand, tape, italic, copperplate, poster, ornamental and drawing, and mapping.

INKS
Water- or acrylic-based inks are used. Chinese sumi inks are the most popular.

PAPER
This can be anything from simple photocopier paper to heavier stock. Layout paper is good to have on hand for tracing purposes.

SLOPING BOARD
It is advisable to work on a sloping board (tilted at an angle) when writing calligraphy.

PAPER & TYPE

Paper & type is run by graphic designer Victoria Vu (see also pages 24 and 168). She works with clients to create one-of-a-kind designs as well as a stationery line consisting of greeting cards and notebooks. Inspired by florals, calligraphy, and simple typography, Vu likes to make products that encourage correspondence for both everyday and significant occasions.

Her Thanks So Much card combines calligraphy with hand-drawn illustrations, while her How Are You card takes advantage of the loopy nature of calligraphy. The calligraphy for both cards was done using India ink and a medium-sized writing nib.

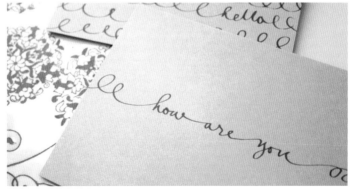

PAPERFINGER

BROOKLYN, NEW YORK, USA

Bryn Chernoff of Paperfinger specializes in modern calligraphy, unique hand lettering, and illustration to produce anything from invitations to logos and branding, rubber stamps, tattoos, and stationery. Chernoff always works with a pen on paper, employing traditional calligraphy tools such as nibs and dip pens for different effects. She then scans her work for reproduction as needed.

Shown here are her Choose Your Greeting holiday card and Thank You card, alongside some of her ready-made and customized stamp sets.

K IS FOR
CALLIGRAPHY

MORAGA, CALIFORNIA, USA

Designer and calligrapher Katy Jamison runs this calligraphy and handmade craft business, producing greeting cards, gift tags, envelope seals, and other calligraphic art objects. She creates her unique lettering using Brause 361 Steno pointed nibs with vintage nib-holders, together with either black Moon Palace sumi ink, acrylic ink, or Winsor and Newton gouache.

Jamison has developed nineteen different lettering styles, and the items shown here feature lettering derived from two of these—her Bend it like Bickham and Con Tiempo.

MEANT TO BE
CALLIGRAPHY
AND FIG 2 DESIGN

WASHINGTON, D.C. /
BETHESDA, MARYLAND, USA

This series of cards is the result of
a collaboration between Michele
Hatty Fritz of Meant To Be Calligraphy
and stationery designer Claudia
Smith of Fig 2 Design. The cards
feature a combination of type set
in Chalet Comprime and Fritz's
hand-drawn calligraphy.

"Claudia asked me to use my
signature style to put my own spin
on three phrases: Thanks for Bringing
Sexy Back, Get Your Groove On, and
You Rock My World," explains Fritz.
"I looked at each phrase separately
and then tried to make each flow
together in a cohesive way."

Fritz used a Brause EF 66 nib to create
the lettering. The cards were then
letterpress sprinted using fluorescent
inks on 100 percent Crane's Lettra
Fluorescent White cardstock.

FAWNSBERG

LYNDONVILLE, VERMONT, USA

Fawnsberg is the stationery side of the already established modern, whimsical calligraphy company, Primele. It is run by sisters Patricia and Rachel Mumau. "We love letter writing and have devoted the launch of Fawnsberg to letter sheets," explains Patricia. "Our vision is that others will use our papers to write to loved ones without occasion—merely to say hello, reflect on the day, perhaps express thoughts that they've had. We hope to encourage people to celebrate the 'everyday.'"

Their I Often Think of You and For You I Pine cards both feature contemporary calligraphy. The lettering for the Often card was created using pointed pen, while the For You I Pine lettering was created using pencil before being scanned and redrawn using a graphics tablet.

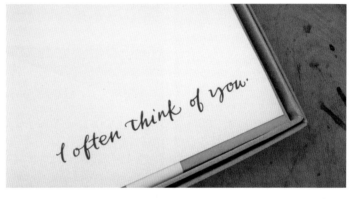

THE LEFT HANDED CALLIGRAPHER

DALLAS, TEXAS, USA

The Left Handed Calligrapher is Nicole Black. Almost everything she makes is created by hand using ink on paper, and she specializes in pointed-pen calligraphy.

These two greeting cards combine calligraphy with Black's hand-drawn illustrations. The holiday card was created using sumi ink and a Gillott 303 nib; it was printed on Strathmore Writing 80lb Cover Bristol paper. The design for the Thank You card was made using Prismacolor watercolor pencils and was printed on the same paper.

PLURABELLE CALLIGRAPHY

LOS ANGELES, CALIFORNIA, USA

Plurabelle Calligraphy is run by Molly Suber Thorpe. Thorpe uses a number of vintage calligraphic styles and modern styles of her own creation. Many of her letterforms are based on traditional styles—such as Copperplate and Spencerian—but these are then combined with modern layouts and color palettes to create a contemporary feel.

Thorpe created the lettering for these stamps using a pointed pen with black ink on white paper. This was then scanned and cleaned up in Photoshop.

The gift tags feature Thorpe's own lettering creation, Tigerlily, a Copperplate-inspired contemporary alphabet, written using a Brause 66EF pointed steel nib.

CHAPTER 7

PAPERCUTTING

The art of papercutting and paper crafting as a whole has seen a considerable rise in popularity in recent years, but it has been in existence since as far back as the sixth century.

Papercutting is an ancient form of folk art and its history lies in China, where the art is known as *jian zhi*. Long traditions in papercutting exist in other countries too, including *kirie* in Japan, *sanjhi* in India, and the famous *papel picados* in Mexico.

Creatives working in this medium use a number of different techniques. Some cut straight into a chosen paper, essentially drawing with their cutting tool. Others first sketch or print out their design and then cut around its marked-out lines. Tools may include scissors, scalpels, or other forms of blade.

Most papercutters tend to start each new piece by cutting out the most difficult parts first, before moving on to the rest of the artwork. Curved areas are best cut with a swift, confident movement; angular areas with shorter stabbing motions. Another good tip is to cut toward yourself and rotate the artwork on a table to make that possible. This is not practical when working on large pieces but works well for smaller pieces.

Once a papercut is complete it is advisable to mount it. This can be as simple as mounting it onto another piece of paper, either plain or colored, or onto a heavier stock. In cases where a design has been cut directly into a greeting card or notebook cover, a sheet of paper can be inserted behind the cut to add depth and color. Laser cutting is also an option if an original papercut design is to be produced in large numbers.

PAPERCUTTING TOOLS

PAPER

It is best to use a light- to medium-weight paper when cutting more intricate, detailed designs, but for simpler designs a heavier stock can be used. As a general rule, try not to use a highly textured stock as the fibers in the paper will drag when you cut it.

X-ACTO KNIFE

A brand of scalpel popular among papercutters.

SCALPEL

Also known as a lancet, a scalpel is a sharp, steel-bladed instrument used for cutting. Scalpels are either disposable or have replaceable blades.

CRAFT MAT

Otherwise known as a self-healing mat, this is important as it protects both the work surface and your blade and provides a solid base on which to work.

ASHLEY PAHL DESIGN
∙∙∙∙∙∙∙∙∙∙∙∙∙∙∙∙∙∙∙∙∙∙∙∙∙∙∙∙∙∙∙
NAPERVILLE, ILLINOIS, USA

Crafter and maker Ashley Pahl used papercutting to create this selection of cards. "I love creating simple designs in clean silhouettes," she explains. "Patterns from nature, such as woodgrain, topography, or even animal forms are most common in my line, often with a little lace or ruffle to bring back that element of celebration. I prefer to work with brown packaging paper, brown cardstock, and twine, since they have a very natural look, and are usually made from recycled materials."

Pahl first sketches out her designs in pencil before using a craft knife to cut along her penciled lines. She then uses a vinyl eraser to get rid of any lingering pencil marks.

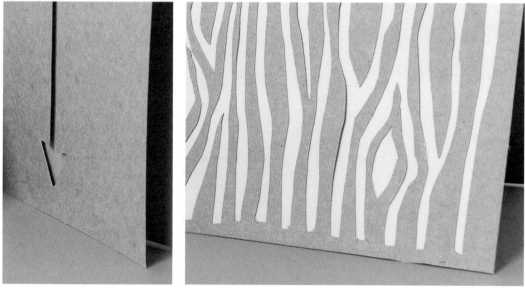

RUBY WREN DESIGNS

KETTERING,
NORTHAMPTONSHIRE, UK

This small business is based in a small town in Northamptonshire. "We work to create products as greenly and as ethically as possible, while aiming to be stylish and unique," explains founder Hayley Mitchell. "Our main line consists of designs hand cut into Ellie Poo paper, which is made from 100 percent postconsumer waste and elephant poo. I love working with this stock—the natural texture gives a beautiful rustic effect and the off-white color of the recycled paper looks stunning in contrast to the bright colors that show through the hand-cut shapes on our cards."

These greeting cards were inspired by birds, animals, wildlife, and nature in general. Each was hand cut using a scalpel and colored paper was then glued to the inside.

HELLO JENUINE

DUNDEE, ANGUS, UK

Illustrator Jen Collins of Hello Jenuine works mainly in pencil, ink, and watercolors (see also page 56). Shown here is her papercut Thank You card.

"I wanted to try a new tool for making a card design. Since I print a lot of my work, I wanted to try my hand at laser cutting to create a simple but effective design," she explains. "After creating the hand-drawn lettering design, the card was then laser cut at my local print studio, where visitors are allowed to use the machine themselves to work on personal projects. Once the design was cut, a layer of paper was applied inside the card, adding color and emphasizing the papercut design."

The card was created using 100 percent recycled card and Murano paper.

SAKURA SNOW

AMSTERDAM,
THE NETHERLANDS

Shown here are a series of papercut cards designed by Suzanne Norris of Sakura Snow (see also page 62).

Created as seasonal greeting cards, these were inspired by Japanese kirigami as well as other folk-art papercutting traditions. "I began by doodling ideas in my sketchbook, then made a couple of prototypes to figure out sizing, positioning, and color combinations," Norris explains. "Once these initial decisions were made, and the card and paper were selected and purchased, I began the process of cutting and constructing the cards."

Each card was made from 220gsm card from Rössler Papier's Paperado line.

HEART ZEENA

LONDON, UK

These papercut letter cards are by Zeena Shah of heart zeena (see also page 48). "I wanted to create something really special, personal, and unique using papercutting," she says. "I first created a series of drawings, chose one to work from, then cut into it. Things often change as I cut—what I really love about papercutting is that no two items are ever the same."

Shah then likes to finish her cards with extra details; these ones have stitched spines.

SKINNY LAMINX

CAPE TOWN, SOUTH AFRICA

Heather Moore is the textile-designing creative behind Skinny laMinx, a company that produces screen-printed pillows, dishcloths, and aprons, as well as a line of fabrics.

Moore also creates a number of paper items, examples of which are these papercut gift tags and card. These were created by first drawing the bird images onto white paper, taping them to double-sided card, and then cutting out the images using an NT cutter blade.

The images were scanned and traced in Adobe Illustrator. Moore then gave the digital files to a laser cutter who could produce the cards and tags in larger numbers.

The stock used is a firm brown card known as Cape Liner.

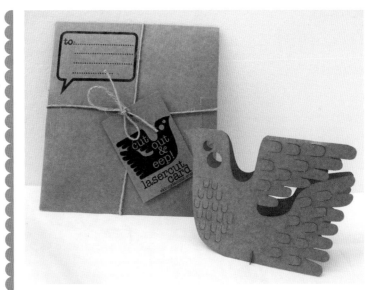

MRYEN

··

LEEDS, WEST YORKSHIRE, UK

Designer and papercutter Jonathan Chapman, otherwise known as MrYen, creates both personal and commissioned works, from artworks to notebooks to cards. This is a selection of some of his hand-cut paper notebooks. The vintage map notebooks feature his typography and are made from found vintage maps. Each was hand bound.

The geometric series of notebooks, also hand bound, were cut with a scalpel. Each page was also rounded using a corner-cutting tool.

The notes series, again, features Chapman's hand-cut typography, set in Lobster with the braces in Baskerville.

Each of the four notepads features either crossed, lined, dotted, or gridded paper.

PAINTED FISH STUDIO
••••••••••••••••••••••••••••••••
MINNEAPOLIS, MINNESOTA,
USA

Painted Fish Studio is run by Jen
Shaffer, who makes stationery goods
and gifts. These are some of her
punched cards and notebooks.

Each card is designed digitally before
a template is printed out and then
used for guiding the punching.
Shaffer uses a Japanese bookbinding
drill to create the holes that make up
the letters and words on both cards
and notebooks.

"I would like to think that people who
buy my paper goods are those who
value aspects of a slower way of life:
instead of texting or sending an
e-mail, they prefer to send a letter,"
she says. "Rather than uploading all
their photos online, they're having
them printed and stored in a
handmade photo album. They're
writing their thoughts in a journal,
not in a blog."

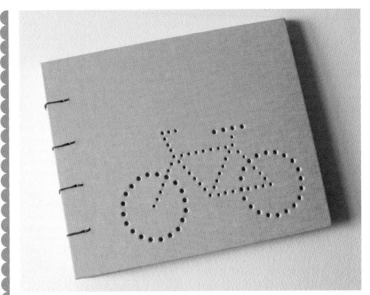

MADE BY JULENE

WORTHING, WEST SUSSEX, UK

Made by Julene is papercutting artist Julene Harrison's company. She makes handmade papercuts to order—from invitations to cards to letterheads—in her distinctive illustrative and typographic style.

"Originally a constructed textile designer, I have now started papercutting. It's a medium I have quickly grown to love," she explains. "I get a lot of pleasure turning a single sheet of paper into something people seem to enjoy."

Harrison starts her designs in rough in Adobe Photoshop, working out a layout and sketching details of more specific elements. She then prints out her rough design ready for the cutting process, for which she uses a scalpel.

CHAPTER 8

COLLAGE / 3-D / SEWN

Creating artwork for stationery goods using mixed media is becoming increasingly widespread. From collage to origami to stitching and sewing, there are many ways to bring greeting cards, journals, or other stationery items to life.

Collage in all its forms—from paper and card only, to paper, beads, stamps, and more—is a great way to create a journal or greeting card with a handmade aesthetic. Using found ephemera to create collage has the additional benefit of using materials that would otherwise be discarded.

Origami is the traditional Japanese art of paper folding. Steeped in history, it remains popular and is increasingly used by crafters and designers. Using it in its flatter form— modular origami—allows stationery designers to add a 3-D element to a piece while keeping it practical and usable.

Sewing or stitching imagery, lettering, or patterns directly onto paper or card is often used to distinguish an otherwise simple design, and offers opportunities for experimentation. Some designers sew or stitch freehand, while others draw out a design and follow it; some even punch holes in the paper or card through which to pass their thread.

The best thread is embroidery floss, which is of good quality, comes in a huge variety of colors, and is strong enough to withstand being pulled through cardstock. A sewing machine can also be used to create patterns or imagery or to secure other materials to a card or journal cover.

COLLAGE / 3-D / SEWN TOOLS

PAPER AND CARD
Paper choice is dependent on the type of project. It can be anything from lightweight tissue to heavy cardstock.

FABRIC
As with paper, the use and choice of fabric is dependent on the project.

NEEDLES
Needles must be sharp enough to be able to push through whatever stock is being used.

PUNCHES
Not just hole punches but also hearts, flowers, larger circles, and more—punches are crafters' essential tools.

THREAD
Embroidery floss is the most popular thread due to its quality and versatility.

GLUE
Crafters tend to work with water-based PVA glue, as it is nontoxic, dries clear, and works with many different materials.

MOD PODGE
An all-in-one glue, sealer, and finisher beloved by crafters.

DOUBLE-SIDED TAPE
Popular with crafters as it is easy, quick, and secure.

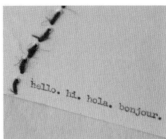

PAPER PATH

WALLA WALLA,
WASHINGTON, USA

Rachel Smith works under the name of Paper Path, creating unique stationery goods using paper, string, colored thread, 3-D objects, and a typewriter. Her cards are made out of heavy watercolor paper or Bristol board. Smith then either adds text, using a 1950s Royal Quiet De Luxe typewriter, or fastens on 3-D elements, such as buttons, poker chips, or letters.

Smith's Cute as a Button new baby card and Love, Hello, Hi, and Happy cards use buttons and Scrabble tiles to spell out their messages. "I love using 3-D objects to add a little more dimensionality to a flat card," she explains. "Finding fun geometric papers and cardstock then adds a flourish of color and helps the letters stand out."

CURIOUS DOODLES

....

PORTLAND, OREGON, USA

Curious Doodles is run by designer Laura Trimmell, who produces a hand-stitched stationery line and Do It Yourself Stitchies packs. "I am trying to promote nondigital, slow communication with my embroidery card kits. Each kit requires my customer to add a bit of themselves with their stitches and the words they write inside. The finished product is oh-so-tactile and will be treasured far longer than a mass-produced card."

Each card and card pack is made up of recycled paper and high-quality embroidery floss. "I originally started creating hand-stitched cards for my loved ones, and they were so well received I decided to expand the line to make them available for my customers," says Trimmell.

A QUICK STUDY

PHILADELPHIA,
PENNSYLVANIA, USA

Zoe Rooney is the designer behind
A Quick Study, and produces paper
goods dedicated to the tradition of
handwritten communication. "While
I love blogging and the Internet, I don't
think there's any comparison with
writing down messages, thoughts,
and ideas longhand on paper," she
explains. "I've been creating paper
goods for a while but recently I've
been focusing on embroidered paper.
I love the tactile aspects of perforating
the paper using an awl, then pulling
the needle and thread through to
create designs."

Rooney drew these designs in pencil
before using an awl to perforate the
cardstock with evenly spaced holes
along the lines of the letters. She then
stitched two strands of embroidery
floss through the holes. The stitches
Rooney uses most often are back
stitch and chain stitch.

BUNNYFUZZ DESIGNS

....

KANSAS CITY, MISSOURI,
USA

Bunnyfuzz Designs is run by Molly Ralston, who creates her stationery goods using mainly felt, paper, and thread, and sometimes buttons. "I am inspired by nature, and particularly love clouds. My best ideas are often pretty random ones and I tend to create spontaneously when just the right idea strikes me," she explains. "My clients are those who still appreciate 'snail mail' and are looking for something unique to send."

Each of these cards was created by hand. Ralston used textured card and then lined each with a smoother stock more suitable for writing on. "Hand-stitching adds a quality that can't be replicated by a machine," she adds. "It also allows me to stitch in greater detail."

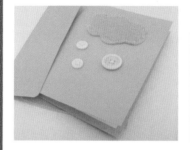

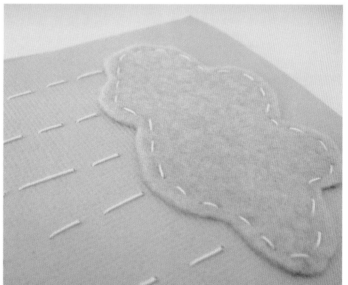

POLKADOTSHOP

TAMPA, FLORIDA, USA

Tammy Lombardi is the crafter and maker behind polkadotshop. She creates greeting cards, gift tags, and other paper goods by sewing on paper or fabric and mixing in hand-drawn details. "I enjoy using different colors and textures in my work," she explains. " I love drawing and my special sketchbook—full of drawings and sketches of all the places I have visited—is my main source of inspiration."

Shown here are her stitched Owl and Tasty Cupcake cards and Bunting Banner gift tags. Each one features the use of collage using paper, card, or fabric with additional features added in either ribbon, chalk, or cotton thread stitches.

MR.PS
....

MANCHESTER, LANCASHIRE,
UK

Mr.PS was set up and is run by designer and illustrator Megan Price. As well as paper goods she produces housewares and artworks. All goods in her lines have a distinctive handmade aesthetic, with the use of bright colors and bold text, which take inspiration from vintage signage and British traditions.

Her card line was developed with old-fashioned communication methods in mind. "Today our friendships tend to be scattered around the country and the world. We stay in touch digitally and remotely; by e-mail, Facebook, Twitter," says Price. "While these methods are to be embraced there is something quite joyous about receiving a printed card with a handwritten message."

The letters for each of these cards were screen printed and then cut out and fixed to the cards with glue dots.

COOKIE CUTTER

SINGAPORE

Cookie Cutter is run by Sandy Ng, who loves working with her hands. "Most of the time you'll find me hanging out with my sewing machine in the little work area in my apartment," she explains. "I am deeply in love with Japanese cotton linen but my love for textures extends to paper as well."

Intrigued by the idea of sewing on paper, Ng created this series of notecards. She started by creating the digital artwork and printing the writing lines before machine-sewing each card's border. She then embroidered "Hello" and finished each one off by sewing on two buttons. Ng used a thick, white, textured paper stock that would hold the weight of the buttons and would not tear when sewn.

REWORK STUDIO

ROCHESTER, NEW YORK, USA

Rework Studio is run by graphic designer Dezirae Moore and came about after many years of playing with paper. "As a graphic designer with an itch for the insanely detailed and handmade, I've maintained a variety of hobbies, most of which incorporate hand lettering, calligraphy, and bookbinding. Most recently, these hobbies have meshed together and resulted in the hand-stitched letters and designs on paper that I make for Rework Studio."

Shown here are Moore's hand-stitched greeting cards. The design for each originated with hand-drawn lettering or artwork that was then transferred onto precut and scored paper. Sewing holes were punched and then each card was individually sewn by hand. "I love the idea of marrying paper and string together to help bring the design off the paper. The texture of the string on paper is surprising yet pleasing," says Moore.

PAPER & TYPE

LOS ANGELES, CALIFORNIA, USA

This greeting card was made by graphic designer Victoria Vu of paper & type (see also pages 24 and 136). It was created for Valentine's Day but it can be used at any time of year and for any reason.

"I'd been getting into sewing at the time I created this card so had an array of red patterned fabrics. These inspired the eclectic mix of sewn hearts," explains Vu. "My plan was to keep the design simple and the message subtle enough for it to be used at any time."

For you, lots of these.

LIZZIMARIE

APPLETON, WISCONSIN, USA

Lizzimarie is run by creative crafter Liz Tubman, who enjoys lots of different art forms, including hand-printed and stitched artwork, stationery, and paper goods. "I strive to create unique, handmade, and inspiring pieces that you wouldn't be able to find in a large store," she explains. "I love to create and my goal is to impart that love and inspiration to anyone who comes through my shop."

Shown here are her handcrafted, recycled yellow and blue Bunting notebooks, Japanese-bound Notes notebook, stitched Pinwheel card, and stitched Hello cards.

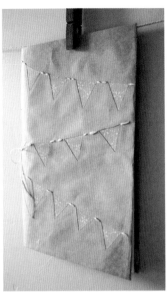

TOKYO CRAFTS

SEATTLE, WASHINGTON, USA

Miki Bloch is the designer and artist behind stationery company Tokyo Crafts. Originally from Tokyo, she now lives in Seattle, where she both runs her company and teaches Japanese art.

"The traditional Japanese technique of origami is my lifelong passion," she explains. "I love to make unique and lovely items. I fold any type of origami you can imagine—including 'modular origami' (also known as 3-D origami)—and make everything with high-quality paper from Japan."

These greeting cards feature her handcrafted origami shapes and characters, including a dachshund and a bulldog.

SARA BALCOMBE

EDMONTON, ALBERTA,
CANADA

Sara Balcombe is a designer by day and a paper crafter by night. "I like making pretty things and I like doing it in a different way," she explains. "I like taking ordinary tools and, rather than using them for what they were originally intended, I like to use them to make something completely unexpected."

These greeting cards were created using a number of different materials and techniques, including stamps, punches, glue, and chalk pastels mixed with water. "I love stamps and punches because they give you a lovely uniformity to work with," she says. "I also use chalk pastel for color. I use it like paint—you can get really excellent shades and opacities simply by adding less or more water."

CAMPBELL RAW PRESS

·······································

NEW YORK, NEW YORK, USA

Shown here is the work of bookbinder and letterpress printer Maggie Campbell of Campbell Raw Press. She specializes in decorative, exposed bindings and uses a variety of materials, including silk, linen, and cotton cloths, Japanese silk-screened and stenciled papers, acid-free papers, linen thread, ribbons, and vintage stamps.

A major feature of these journals and albums is their distinctive sewn spines. They are made using the "coptic stitch" structure, which is both elegant and sturdy. They feature acid-free materials, including *chiyogami* (Japanese silk-screened papers), bookboard, printmaking papers, and waxed linen thread.

"It's very important to me to create beautiful, unique work that is also functional, lasting, and elegant," explains Campbell. "I want people to enjoy my books for many generations to come."

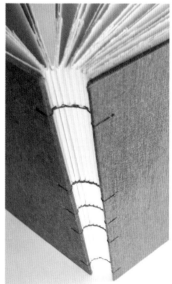

BY BELINDA

....

LOS ANGELES, CALIFORNIA, USA

By Belinda is owned and run by Belinda Vong. She specializes in hand-embroidered paper art and greeting cards. "I value celebrating the everyday and sharing with people just how special they are to you," she explains. "I create cards that aren't going to be lost in a sea of other cards, get shoved into a box and put away, or tossed into the trash. Instead, they are to be treasured as a piece of art."

Each card she creates starts with an image or a phrase. Vong then hand draws the image onto the card before stitching it. She uses only white thread on colored card. The text is typed out on an electronic typewriter, cut out, and then glued in place.

HAVE & HOLD DESIGN
....

TORONTO, ONTARIO
CANADA

These cards are from the Celebrate!
collection by designer Samantha
Dubeau (see also page 104).
Each one was handcrafted and
is truly unique.

The cards feature crepe streamers,
ribbons, cupcake liners, thread, and
various bits of colored paper. "I collaged,
punched the confetti, and cut the
fringe by hand. I jumped on the sewing
machine a few times too," Dubeau
explains. "I like to mix things up by
incorporating unexpected techniques
and elements. It makes the pieces all
the more dynamic."

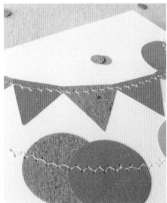

DOGSRULE

....

VERNON, NEW JERSEY, USA

Janice Lagard of dogsrule is a designer and crafter who specializes in paper goods using the Japanese art of origami. "I like the crispness of the paper folds and the intricate designs that are created from the precise folding and layering," she explains.

The card and gift tags shown here feature origami medallions that were created using a technique sometimes known as "tea bag" folding. They were made using eight hand-cut pieces of French paper that were folded to create a 3-D effect. Lagard then affixed them to the card and tags and gently "lifted" them to add to the effect.

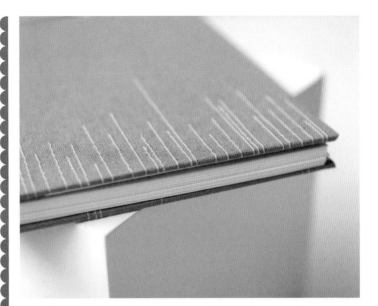

ONE FINE DAE

SEATTLE, WASHINGTON, USA

Shown here are the Remember This album and The City Sleeps notebook by Linda-Thuan Pham (see also page 121). "I've always loved a good notebook and carry one with me everywhere, so it's what I specialize in," she explains. "I'm drawn to simple and modern aesthetics with a dash of vintage charm. I like feeling nostalgic and I hope that my pieces will provoke that same feeling in my customers."

The artwork for these two pieces was created digitally and then printed onto the back of a sheet of book cloth. Pham then used a sewing machine to stitch over the printed design; what you see on the finished product is the front of the book cloth. "I always like to add a bit of texture to my books, to have some sort of tactile feedback," Pham says. "The threaded lines are subtle, yet add detail to the overall design and respond to you when you run your fingers over them."

RESOURCES

SUPPLIERS

PAPER

Alexander Paper Supplies
www.alexanderpapersupplies.co.uk

Antalis
www.antalis.co.uk

California Paper Goods
www.californiapapergoods.com

Crane & Co.
www.crane.com

eco-craft
www.eco-craft.co.uk

The Exotic Paper Company
www.elliepoopaper.co.uk

Finch Paper
www.finchpaper.com

French Paper Company
www.frenchpaper.com

Green Paper Company
www.greenpapercompany.com

Hahnemühle Fine Art
www.hahnemuhledirect.com

JPP (John Purcell Paper)
www.johnpurcell.net

K.W.Doggett Fine Paper
www.kwdoggett.com.au

Kate's Paperie
www.katespaperie.com

Keldon Paper
www.keldonpaper.com

Kelly Paper
www.kellypaper.com

Lawrence Art Supplies
www.lawrence.co.uk

Legion Paper
www.legionpaper.com

Letterpress Paper
www.letterpresspaper.com

The Paper Mill Store
www.thepapermillstore.com

Paper Presentation
www.paperpresentation.com

Paper Source
www.paper-source.com

R.K. Burt & Company Ltd
www.rkburt.com

Vlieger
www.vliegerpapier.nl

LETTERPRESS

Bison Bookbinding & Letterpress
www.bisonbookbinding.com

Box Car Press
www.boxcarpress.com

Briar Press
www.briarpress.org

British Letterpress
www.britishletterpress.co.uk

Eluma Letterpress Plates
www.letterpressplates.com

Five Roses
www.fiveroses.org

Hamilton Wood Type
& Printing Museum
www.woodtype.org

I Love Letterpress
www.iloveletterpress.com

Ladies of Letterpress
www.ladiesofletterpress.ning.com

Letterpress Alive
www.letterpressalive.co.uk

NA Graphics
www.nagraph.com

SCREEN PRINTING

Adelco
www.adelco.co.uk

Art 2 Screenprint.com
www.art2screenprint.com

D. Roper Ltd
screenprintsupplies.co.uk

London Screen Service
www.londonscreenservice.co.uk

Nehoc Australia
www.nehoc.com.au

Renaissance Graphic Arts, Inc.
www.printmaking-materials.com

Screen Stretch
www.screenstretch.co.uk

SilkScreeningSupplies.com
www.silkscreeningsupplies.com

Standard Screen
www.standardscreen.com

Victory Factory
www.victoryfactory.com

Wicked Printing Stuff
www.wickedprintingstuff.com

GENERAL ARTS AND CRAFTS

A.I. Friedman
www.aifriedman.com

Clarkes
www.clarkesonline.co.uk

Clear Bags
www.clearbags.com

Deans Art
www.deansart.com.au

Eckersley's Art & Craft
www.eckersleys.com.au

eco-craft
www.eco-craft.co.uk

Envelopper Inc
www.envelopperinc.com

Liberty
www.liberty.co.uk

Merrypak
www.merrypak.co.za

Mountain Cow
www.mountaincow.com

Neil's Art Store
www.e-artstore.net

New York Central Art Supply
www.nycentralart.com

Oxford Art Supplies
www.oxfordart.com.au

Paperchase
www.paperchase.co.uk

Paper Convention
www.paperconvention.com

Pen to Paper
www.pentopaperonline.com

Peter van Ginkel
www.petervanginkel.nl

Simon's Stamps
www.simonstamp.com

Speedball Art
www.speedballart.com

The Square Envelope Company
www.squareenvelope.com.au

Vlieger
www.vliegerpapier.nl

Waste Not Paper
www.wastenotpaper.com

BLOGS AND ONLINE COMMUNITIES

Craftster
www.craftster.org

The Daily Smudge
thedailysmudge.blogspot.com

Design*Sponge
www.designsponge.com

Designers Toolbox
www.designerstoolbox.com

Etsy
www.etsy.com

FPO: For Print Only
www.underconsideration.com/fpo

Lottie Loves
charlotterivers.blogspot.com

Notes to a Further Excuse
notestoafurtherexcuse.blogspot.com

Oh Joy!
ohjoy.blogs.com

Oh So Beautiful Paper
www.ohsobeautifulpaper.com

Origami Club
www.en.origami-club.com

Paper Craft Planet
www.papercraftplanet.com

Paper Crave
www.papercrave.com

Poppytalk
poppytalk.blogspot.com

Print & Pattern
printpattern.blogspot.com

Printeresting
www.printeresting.org

Printspecs
print-specs.blogspot.com

Pushing Papers
www.pushing-papers.com

Save Gocco
www.savegocco.com

Snap + Tumble
snapandtumble.blogspot.com

Typoretum
blog.typoretum.co.uk

Uppercase
uppercase.squarespace.com

TRADE SHOWS

Autumn Fair International
www.autumnfair.com

Brooklyn Flea
www.brooklynflea.com

The Finders Keepers
www.thefinderskeepers.com

Hong Kong International Stationery Fair
www.hktdc.com/fair/hkstationeryfair-en

Life Instyle
www.lifeinstyle.com.au

National Stationery Show
www.nationalstationeryshow.com

New York International Gift Fair
www.nyigf.com

Printsource New York
www.printsourcenewyork.com

Progressive Greetings Live:
The London International Card Show
www.progressivegreetingslive.co.uk

Pulse
www.pulse-london.com

Reed Gift Fairs
www.reedgiftfairs.com.au

Renegade Craft Fair
www.renegadecraft.com

Spring Fair International
www.springfair.com

Stationery Show
www.stationeryshow.co.uk

Surtex
www.surtex.com

Top Drawer London
www.topdrawer.co.uk

CONTRIBUTOR DETAILS

1canoe2
www.1canoe2.com

Acute & Obtuse
acuteandobtuse.com

Akimbo
www.akimbo.com.au

Allison Cole Illustration
www.allisoncoleillustration.com

Alyssa Nassner
www.alyssanassner.com

amymarcella
www.amymarcella.etsy.com

Andy Pratt
www.andypratt.net

Anja Jane
www.anjajane.com

Anna Fewster / Lampyridae Press
www.annafewster.co.uk

Ashley Pahl Design
www.ashleypahl.com

Brie Harrison
www.briedee.com

Bunnyfuzz Designs
www.bunnyfuzz.etsy.com

By Belinda
bybelinda.etsy.com

Cabin + Cub
www.cabinandcub.com

Campbell Raw Press
www.brooklynbookbinder.com

Cody Haltom
codyhaltom.com

Cookie Cutter
cookiecutteretsy.etsy.com

Corrupiola
corrupiola.com.br

cricicis design
www.cricicisdesign.com

Curious Doodles
www.curiousdoodles.etsy.com

Darling Clementine
www.darlingclementine.no

Dependable Letterpress
www.dependableletterpress.com

dogsrule
www.dogsrule.etsy.com

Drawcity
www.drawcity.etsy.com

DWRI Letterpress
dwriletterpress.net

Egg Press
www.eggpress.com

enormouschampion
enormouschampion.com

Fawnsberg
fawnsberg.myshopify.com

Field Guide Design
fieldguide35.blogspot.com

Fig 2 Design
www.fig2design.com

Flowermill
www.flowermill.co.za

Galison
www.galison.com

Gemma Correll
www.gemmacorrell.com

Gigi Gallery
www.gigigallery.etsy.com

Good On Paper Design
www.goodonpaperdesign.com

Hammerpress
hammerpress.net

Have & Hold Design
www.haveandholddesign.com

Heart Zeena
zeenashah.com

Heidi Burton
heidiburton.co.uk

Hello Jenuine
www.hellojenuine.com

The Hungary Workshop
thehungryworkshop.com.au

Igloo Letterpress
iglooletterpress.com

The Indigo Bunting
indigobuntingshop.bigcartel.com

INK + WIT
www.inkandwit.com

Jesse Breytenbach
www.jessebreytenbach.co.za

JHill Design
www.jhilldesign.co.uk

Jill Bliss
jillbliss.com

Jo Clark Design
www.joclarkdesign.co.uk

Joie Studio
www.joiestudio.com

K is for Calligraphy
www.kisforcalligraphy.etsy.com

Karolin Schnoor
www.karolinschnoor.com

Katharine Watson
www.katharinewatson.com

Kirtland House Press
www.kirtlandhouse.com

Kristin Carlson
www.kristincarlson.net

la rara
www.la-rara.com

The Left Handed Calligrapher
www.thelefthandedcalligrapher.com

Lizzimarie
www.lizzimarie.etsy.com

Lox+Savvy
www.loxsavvy.com.au

Lucy King
www.lucykingdesign.com

Made by Julene
madebyjulene.com

Mai Autumn
maiautumn.com

Mary & Gabrielle Events
maryandgabrielle.com

May Day Studio
www.maydaystudio.com

me and amber
www.meandamber.com

Meant To Be Calligraphy
www.meanttobecalligraphy.com

Melanie Linder
www.melanielinderillustration.com

Merry Day
merryday.etsy.com

Morris & Essex
www.morrisessex.com

Mr.PS
www.mr-ps.co.uk

MrYen
www.mr-yen.com

Nancy & Betty Studio
www.nancyandbetty.com

Natasha Mileshina / bubbo
www.bubbo.etsy.com

Nora Whynot Paper Goods
www.norawhynot.com.au

O-Check Design Graphics
(Spring come, rain fall)
www.o-check.net

Oh My Deer Handmades
www.ohmydeer.etsy.com

Old Tom Foolery
www.oldtomfoolery.com

One Fine Dae
onefinedae.etsy.com

Painted Fish Studio
paintedfishstudio.com

paper & type
www.paperandtype.com

Paper Path
www.etsy.com/shop/paperpath

Paperfinger
www.paperfinger.com

Papersheep Press
www.papersheeponline.com

Pine Street Makery
www.etsy.com/shop/
pinestreetmakery

Planet Press
www.planetpress.biz

Plurabelle Calligraphy
plurabellecalligraphy.com

polkadotshop
www.etsy.com/shop/polkadotshop

Poppies Flowers
poppiesflowers.com.au

Present & Correct
www.presentandcorrect.com

Primele
primele.com

Publique Living
www.publiqueliving.com

A Quick Study
aquickstudyonline.com

REDSTAR ink
www.redstarink.com

Rework Studio
www.etsy.com/shop/reworkstudio

Ruby Victoria Letterpress
& Printmaking
www.rubyvictoria.etsy.com

Ruby Wren Designs
www.rubywren.com

Sakura Snow
www.sakurasnow.com

Sara Balcombe
sarabalcombe.com

Satsuma Press
www.satsumapress.com

Scout Books
www.scoutbooks.com

Scout Books
www.scoutbooks.com

Seesaw Designs
www.seesawdesigns.com

Sesame Letterpress
www.sesameletterpress.com

Shanna Murray
shannamurray.com

Shop Toast
www.toast-ed.com

Skinny laMinx
www.skinnylaminx.com

Smock Paper
smockpaper.com

Snap + Tumble
snapandtumble.com

Spring Olive
springolive.com

Sukie
www.sukie.co.uk

Sunlight on Closed Lids
www.sunlightonclosedlids.co.uk

Swiss Cottage Designs
www.swisscottagecustomdesign.com

Thereza Rowe
www.therezarowe.com

These Are Things
thesearethings.com

Tokyo Crafts
www.tokyocrafts.etsy.com

Tuesday Designs
www.tuesdaydesigns.com.au

Vertallee Letterpress
www.vertallee.com

W+K Studio Goodness
wkstudio.bigcartel.com

Will Bryant
willbryant.com

Winged Wheel
www.winged-wheel.co.jp/en/store.html

Wit & Whistle
www.witandwhistle.etsy.com

INDEX

ACKNOWLEDGMENTS

Researching and writing this book was really enjoyable. The countless packages of gorgeous stationery I received for review made me very happy, but they also made for a really tough selection process. I'd like to thank all the designers and crafters who sent work to me. I just wish I could have included it all!

Again, special thanks to the team at RotoVision for their continued design and editorial support.

This book is for Mum, Daniel, and Louis.